married
Beyond Recognition

married
Beyond Recognition

A Humorous Look at Marriage

Sylvia Harney

Unless otherwise noted, all Scripture quotations are from the
New King James Version of the Bible © 1984 by Thomas Nelson,
Inc., Nashville, Tennessee, and are used by permission.

Morning Times Press
1231 NW Broad, Suite 114, Murfreesboro, TN 37129

Printed in the United States of America.

Library of Congress Cataloging-in-Publication Data

Harney, Sylvia.
    Married beyond recognition.

    1. Marriage—Humor.   I. Title.

PN6231.M3H37   1988   818'.5402   88-17358
ISBN 0-943497-25-6

3rd Printing 1997
4th Printing 1998
5th Printing 2001

This book is lovingly and joyfully dedicated to Hank.

Thank you for your love, encouragement, patience,
and that wonderful, well-developed sense of humor.
And I think you are handsome . . .
even if you don't look like Tom Selleck!

CONTENTS

ACKNOWLEDGMENTS.

To Momma and Daddy, known for some forty-three years as Mr. and Mrs. James L. Harney: Thank you for the wonderful, sometimes wacky, always loving, home you created; and even above that for not giving up on your own marriage.

To my brothers, Rodney and Jim, and my "baby" sister, Miriam: I am more than blessed to have experienced growing up with you and having had the delightful privilege of watching your marriages and babies grow.

To Chris: Thank you for your flexibility and patience while I was writing this book, and for being willing to eat almost anything (although I can't remember that *ever* being a problem); for being such an "interesting" teen-ager (you, the reader, will find out what "interesting" means later on in this book).

To my special friends Sara, Janet, Linda, Ann, Leta, Carlene, Judy, Frances, Rachael, Beverly, Sandy, and Lynn: Thank you for having marriages that have endured and for listening patiently while I read my manuscript to you, for laughing at all the right places (usually), for praying for me, and for occasionally checking in on me to make sure I was still alive.

To my editor, George Grant: Thank you for allowing me the sheer joy and discipline of performing one of the most rewarding tasks of my life—my first book! Thank you all for encouraging me and believing in me. I have never known more positive, uplifting, professional people. You and your marriages are an inspiration.

To my heavenly Father: Thank you for being faithful to Your Word. You are truly the God You declare Yourself to be. Thank You for life itself—now and hereafter.

To you, the reader: It is my desire for you and your marriage that you will learn to ignore the nit-picky qualities in your marriage so that you can appreciate the good qualities, and that you might discover new joy every day—and laugh every chance you get.

CONFESSIONS OF A LITERARY WIDOWER

by Hank Widick

Writing about someone, especially the one you love and with whom you share your life, is as risky as driving a Suzuki Samari in the Indianapolis 500, but here goes.

As these words clatter from the keys of my typewriter, we are in the "post manuscript/pre-best-seller list" stage in the birth of a book and while I have never personally witnessed a case of post-partum blues, it must be a lot like this.

Sylvia came into my life twelve years ago, B.B. (before book). I was two years into recovery from a failed first marriage and, while the attraction was fierce and mutual, I was determined never again to chance love and commitment.

It didn't take long for me to realize she had some things that I wanted. For those snickering under their breath and looking back at Sylvia's picture on the cover, it's true, I did want those things. In this case, however, I'm speaking of those intangible qualities that make up her character, like her infectious and indominatible power of positive thought and deed; her spirit, which often exceeds the container designed to hold it; her sense of humor and love of laughter; her fierce and unwavering loyalty; and her honesty.

Since you need to get on with the business of reading this book, let's skip over the others to the last and most important of her qualities that I desired for myself—her complete and unconditional faith in Jesus Christ, our Savior and the Son of the living God.

Sylvia has never failed to live up to my image of her, both in our private and public lives. I have at times, however, failed to see past some small problem and realize the image remained untarnished.

In looking back at my list of her endearing qualities, I realize they are also most of the reasons she wrote this book. The God-ordained relationship between woman and man demands an equal and often unequal exchange of these qualities. This relationship is reinforced to a remarkable resiliency by friendship. Sylvia is my buddy. About the only things we don't enjoy doing together are unstopping the commode and shopping for her shoes.

These, of course, are small issues and hardly worth mentioning as I proclaim myself blessed as a husband.

It's all over, Honey—no more pencil hickeys on your fingers, no more bleary eyes and lines running together on pages, no more twelve hour days at your desk, without even taking a shower. You have finished, I still love you, and after a few months of rehabilitation you should be able to remember how to make meatloaf. —*H.W.*

(Dear Hank, I have *never* known how to make meatloaf . . .)
—*S.H.*

IT TAKES
COURAGE

*M*arriage takes a lot of courage. But then so does facing a grizzly bear on a trail in Yellowstone National Park.

Marriage takes a lot of love and determination, especially since you'll be spending at least every other week thinking you married a maniac.

There are times you walk into the bathroom, take a long, half-crazed look in the mirror and say, "I chose to spend the rest of my life with *this* person? I must be crazy!"

I actually made the mistake of saying so to my husband once in the heat of battle. I opened my mouth and with all the immaturity I could muster I said, "I was crazy when I married you." He quickly replied, "Yeah, and I was so infatuated I didn't notice it!"

If you're one of those types who can only function when everyone marches to your beat, and your home must meet state health inspection regulations for cleanliness—don't get married. And if you do, don't have children. Children hear only the music of their own minds, which, even if we could tap into it, would make no sense to us. Husbands often hear no music at all, which leaves us thinking that some of their parts are missing.

1

"I don't know about you, but we need help!" Most of us think that because we are blissfully in love, when we marry that wonderful person, good things are bound to happen. We think we will in no time parlay our abundant love into abundant riches of the mink coat type, so it comes as a major surprise that we could be so poor . . . for so long.

When I married, my vision was blurred by the here and now: the joy of finding someone I loved—and couldn't imagine being without—blurred by shared interest (with the exception of backpacking). We were both creative people and interested in the other's careers. But little did I know that no one had ever written a marriage guide book for creative persons who marry each other and who wake up one day and can't remember where we put the bills—much less if we paid them.

"Just Thought You Should Know"

"When your spouse gets sick and is miserable, you'll be miserable too! They make sure of that!"

"There's only one crucial stage of marriage. If you can survive this stage you have it made. It's the period immediately following the ceremony until the age of ninety-three. After ninety-three, there's not much left to flap your gums over."

"Marriage is a long trip, so take a lot of rest stops along the way, leave your motor running, and take no detours."

"A lifetime of marriage gives you an honorary degree in patience and endurance. If at anytime you become discouraged and give up, you lose your credentials."

"Marriage requires so much bending and flexing it could be called aerobic exercise."

"A teen-ager stays at least six steps ahead of you and will occasionally turn around to see if you're paying attention."

"One of the biggest ways children can surprise you is by coming into the world when you least expect them."

"Romance is like a paper lantern left standing out in the rain. After a while the light goes out and you're left with a soggy, plain brown bag."

I asked my husband what he thinks about when he's around people who talk too much and he said, "Homicide."

TAKE IT SERIOUSLY, AND LAUGH EVERY CHANCE YOU GET

Expectations

*M*y expectations of marriage were probably a lot like yours—filled with fanciful dreams and practical goals, like marrying someone who looked like Paul Newman (and would age as handsomely). I imagined a man who couldn't breathe without me, who hung on my every word. He would be a man of advanced sensitivities, who would know my thoughts before I spoke them. He would be sentimental without being gushy and would tell everyone that life had no meaning *before* I came along. Remembering our wedding would bring tears to his eyes.

As for finding someone who knows my thoughts before I speak them, well, I can spell out in plain, stripped-down English what's on my mind—and half the time, he still doesn't catch my drift. And the truth is, I'm the one who developed extra sensitivities: just a passing reference to our honeymoon backpacking expedition and I develop a full-blown case of the hives.

My honeymoon was historic. My honeymoon was miserable! I was introduced to the wonderful world of thunderstorms, mosquitoes, and poison ivy. My new husband harbored a lot of dangerous and erroneous beliefs, one of which was that romance could turn a two-man tent into a penthouse suite.

Our marriage got off to a great start from the moment he lifted my backpack onto my tiny little shoulders. I promised myself I would not complain even if I got blisters the size of Arizona on my feet. I hadn't expected to have them on my shoulders as well.

"These shoulder straps are cutting right through my skin."

"Here, let me help," he offered.

"That would be wonderful, but how can you carry two packs?"

He laughed. He's a newlywed and he thinks I'm funny. I'm also a newlywed, and I don't think I'm being funny at all! It was a twenty-two-pound pack that was twenty-two pounds too heavy. I used all my feminine wiles trying to convince him we would not need so many supplies. I was desperate, but he didn't care.

"Don't you think we could leave some of these things at home?" I asked sweetly.

"Like what?"

"Like you and me and the food."

"You're going to love it," he assured me.

"There'll be snakes," I suggested.

"Snakes are much more afraid of you than you are of them."

"I'd like to bring that one up for debate!"

I had been walking in front of him, and we were an hour into our hike up the mountain when he said, "Stop very slowly, turn around, and look down!"

I looked down in the direction of the trail and there it was — a small copperhead stretched out full-length across the trail.

"I just wanted you to see why I asked you to watch where you're going."

"You said, 'snakes are more afraid of us than we are of them.' That fellow doesn't look frightened in the least, and I think I've just had an accident."

I finished the climb up the mountain walking *behind* my new husband. I began an internal debate about which way I wanted to die, by being attacked from behind by a grizzly or from the front by a snake.

We were probably the first backpackers in history to pitch a two-man tent inside an Adirondack-style trail shelter. Since we were protected on three sides, I reasoned that the bears would have only one avenue of attack instead of four. He told me ten years later that the closest bear of any description was 114 miles away in the Smokey Mountains. I figure a bear can cover that distance in five and a half hours, so I am unimpressed even after all these years.

My husband owes several backpacking discoveries directly to me. He discovered that his cooking stove, with five ounces of fuel, will boil just under a gallon of water (one quart at a time), enough to wash a head of shoulder-length blond hair. A daily washing for a week means you only have to carry thirty-five ounces of fuel, a discovery accompanied by the realization that using fuel in this way means you won't be able to cook anything. Cooking didn't matter to me. I was on my honeymoon and fully intended to be looking my best when the rescuers found my body.

He also was naive about the bathroom issue. It does not matter what kind of women we are — the strong, rugged, outdoorsy type or the delicate, ballerina type — we all share a common equality. It's that very fundamental difference between men and women: we cannot stand and deliver.

Struggling into a cold pair of pants in the middle of the night to answer nature's call was not on my entertainment list for a honeymoon. Then, once I was in them, I had to struggle most of the way back out of those same pants. Then I had to balance myself on the balls of my feet, hold onto my clothes, juggle a flashlight and other necessities. I must have resembled an Eastern European circus act last seen on the old "Ed Sullivan Show."

This honeymoon experience was just one of many eye-openers to come that would make me acutely aware of some basic differences between men and women, such as our recollections of past events. For some reason unknown to me we don't recall the same details about our honeymoon. I vividly recall rain, chilling winds, and food that tasted only slightly better than the mud pies I made as a child. He recalls the vitality of the morning air and the view of morning mist rising over the mountain top. The only mist I recall was the kind that turned to mildew in my soggy clothing. He reminisces about the miracle of gourmet food in a pouch, to which you only add water. He claims to have slept like a baby, while I may be still catching up from sleep lost due to the "boulders" beneath my hips.

After that, I told him that the day I learned to survive for a week on beef jerky and be happy smelling like a goat would be the day he takes up needlepoint.

I'm happy to report that I married a man who is willing to compromise. Someone has said that compromise is where both parties get what neither one of them wanted in the first place. That is not necessarily so. I got exactly what I wanted. The backpacking equipment is now collecting dust in the storage shed across town, and since my husband has no desire to take up needlepoint, both of us came up winners. (Except in the kitchen and that's where I've had my revenge.)

The Way to My Husband's Heart Was Not in a Cookbook!

If that old saying, "The way to a man's heart is through his stomach," were true, a lot of us would have been forever single.

I should have suspected something when I was engaged to be married and began receiving wedding gifts. One of the first packages I opened was a set of pots and pans.

"They're so . . . so hard and, oh, a big one, too!" I said, struggling to think of something gracious to say. Little did I realize that one of the girls at the shower was writing down every comment I made, and read them aloud in front of God and my mother as comments I would make on my wedding night.

The sting of that humiliation stayed with me long after the shower. Two good things came from it: I forbid anyone to torture a bride-to-be in that fashion, and I didn't open my mouth on my wedding night.

The first meal I cooked after marriage was a memorable one. I had seen spaghetti and I had eaten spaghetti. It looked simple to me and was the only meal that came to mind as I considered cooking dinner that first day. The way I saw it, spaghetti was a two-step meal. Cooking the pasta was simple enough. It only boiled over three times. After that, I considered emptying the water and spaghetti on top of the stove with all four burners going. It seemed the natural thing to do since it kept boiling over anyway.

I had no earthly idea what went into the spaghetti sauce other than meat and tomatoes. I had observed leaves cooking in a friend's sauce, so I went to the grocery store looking for "some of those leaves." I added fifteen bay leaves (if a little was good, fifteen would be great!) and cooked the sauce for five-and-a-half hours.

I served it. We sliced and ate it. The spaghetti, more like a bay leaf pie, stuck to the roof of our mouths. Overall, the meal left a lasting impression.

The next morning, we woke with a semiterminal virus. Our bodies rejected the spaghetti and it ended up were it should have gone in the first place—flushed!

When the Mexican food craze hit, I thought I had finally found the kind of cuisine that was foolproof. I fixed a fine Mexican dinner; spent three days chopping tomatoes and green onions. My husband had the house fumigated the next day and left me a note that said, "Honey, I think you've discovered a new diet. From now on, let's eat cardboard. It has about the same taste as your corn tortillas, but without the calories."

Eventually, I discovered a new specialty — linguine with clam sauce. I announced to my family that the sauce was top secret. We sat down to eat, and I watched while my family's mouths chewed in slow motion. "I think I've discovered the secret," my husband said. "You cut up old rubber bands in place of the clams." I threatened never to cook again. No one protested.

At this point, you may be thinking that I've never heard of a modern invention known as a cookbook. Some of my friends collect cookbooks. They actually spend *money* on them. And to top it all off, they *read* them. Most of them even cook.

I don't buy cookbooks unless held hostage at gunpoint. All the cookbooks I own were given to me by friends who've had dinner at my house. Not only do I not purchase cookbooks, I can't read them. Most recipes I've read seem as though they were created by a German automotive worker. It's all foreign to me.

The people who annoy me most are those lovely ladies who say, "Oh, this is so easy, so simple. Why, anyone could make this. Absolutely nothing to it."

Invariably, the recipe will read something like "Calibrated, Double-Gauged Chocolate Sauce Over Millie's Modern Miracle Cake." P-L-E-A-S-E-E-E!!! When I look at recipes more than a few lines long, I have a sinking spell for which the only cure is to forget the whole thing.

It's wonderful to have a teen-ager in the house. They'll eat anything. I gave up baking cakes the day I put chocolate icing on a dinner roll and he ate it!

Potluck Nightmares

These days, it seems that you are asked to bring food to everything. Friends have potluck dinners. Church socials announced in the weekly bulletin read, "Please come, enjoy the fellowship, and bring a dish to feed your family and a Third World country."

In the beginning of my married life, I actually prepared dishes for these get-togethers. People would stand around the table picking up their empty casserole dishes. Someone would say, "Does anyone know who brought this, uh, does anyone know *what* this is?" My own husband kept his mouth shut and pretended he had never seen it before. I lost a lot of dishes that way. After the first few dozen dinners, when my dishes went untouched and I was too embarrassed to claim them, I never took food again.

I've witnessed the same phenomenon in a different form whenever the children's choir sings in adult church. The little boy who diligently picks his nose all through the song and the little girl who runs her hand up her dress to parts unknown are *never* claimed at the end of church. To this day, I don't know what happens to them.

My own mother has expressed amazement and surprise at the fact that when in the kitchen, I'm groping in the dark. I had been married eight or ten years before I had the nerve to ask her how to make gravy. She said something properly humiliating like, "Did you grow up in my house, or are you the one raised by a pack of wolves?"

My sister was cooking meals fit for a farmhand by the time she was fourteen. The way I protect myself when the family gathers for large dinners is by pretending that I love to wash dishes. I keep the kitchen cleaned up and don't go anywhere near the stove. Actually it makes for pretty good team work. The truth is, they won't let me near the stove.

I don't know where I was when my mother was cooking. Most likely, curled up reading a good book or off exploring in the woods. No one ever explained to me the importance of learning my way around the kitchen, or that it was possible to harm another human life with my cooking.

Fortunately, I married a wonderful man who began cooking when he was nine years old. He proudly claims to have taught me everything I know about cooking, as well as a few other things.

All We Learned About Sex

If our existence on the face of planet earth had depended on what our mothers knew about sex when they married, most of us wouldn't be here. And if our children's existence had depended on the knowledge our mothers revealed to us about sex, most of our children wouldn't be around either.

When my mother sat me down at age sixteen to talk to me before I went on a date, she stared at me with a look as serious as a heart attack, glanced at the floor, patted my hand, and let the wisdom fly. She said, "Don't hold hands with a boy — it leads to other things." (She will categorically deny this.)

There was a moment of sustained, or was it strained, silence. I already knew what those "other things" were. At that moment, I felt sure she was going to ask me what they were. But the silence won and the teachable moment passed, never to return again. I said that I *knew* what those other things were — not that I had *tried* them! Well, maybe the holding hands part. Never mind the fact that my first kiss had occurred three years earlier on a church hayride. (A church hayride for a group of teen-agers is nothing more than supervised silence.)

If there is any truth to the idea that each generation improves over the last in its openness and ability to deal with what might be called sticky topics, it only takes a second to imagine what my grandmother told my mother when she reached dating age. Nothing!

So it stands to reason that most of life came as a complete surprise to our mothers. My mother has only recently recovered from the shock of rearing four children. She is sixty-something years old and still looks under her bed before turning out the light at night just to be sure that my brother Rodney isn't waiting there to grab her. He scared her so often he added years to her life. Had it not been for Rodney my mother would still be thirty-nine.

My mother comes from a family of five brothers and sisters. I am told that in those days, babies appeared, and no one ever suspected anything (except the mother and father, of course) until the new baby arrived.

When my mother was a child, the old family doctor who delivered all the babies told her that he got the babies from a large hole in a tree across the street. Mother remembers making repeated trips to peer down into that hollow tree. She could never quite figure out why old Dr. Core was the only person who ever found babies there.

Beyond that, the realities of marriage must have come as a complete shock to her. Men and women are created equal, but different, and anyone who denies that needs a refresher course in anatomy and physiology. The differences go deeper than those physical differences which are, "hopefully," immediately noticeable. When it comes to sex, in most cases a man's motor is merely idling, ready at a moment's notice to be put into drive and take off. A woman's engine is more like the car that you dust the snow off of on a cold winter's morning, crank up the engine, then go back in the house to have a second cup of coffee while it warms up! Now, I know what some of you are thinking, and you're right. Sometimes our engines are ready to go *before* that second cup of coffee and it's a good thing. This keeps our husbands on their toes, as well as thoroughly confused as to which move to make next. Anything we can do to gently guide them to that "next move" is always appreciated. This usually involves use of a skill known as communication. Be creative.

Is Your Bra on the Towel Rack for a Reason?

After you marry you have to invent good reasons for things you never gave a second thought about before marriage.

This man I married came out of the bathroom one evening and said, "Is your bra on the towel rack for a reason?"

I was prepared. "Yes, it fits the towel rack better than it does me!"

We don't think about where we put our clothes before marriage, but it can become the subject of a masters thesis afterwards! Even if you have a good reason for hanging your bra on the towel rack, men don't understand. He never hangs *his* clothes on the towel rack. His never get that far off the floor! Most men don't even take the time to throw their clothes on the floor—they just let go and the force of gravity pulls them there.

Now, before my little darlin' rips this page out and threatens me with it, I'd better level with you. Brace yourself. He never puts his clothes on the floor.

For a year after I married my husband, I followed him around the house waiting for him to undress. I followed him around (not for the reason you're thinking) because I thought all men threw their clothes on the floor, and I wanted to be there to catch them before they hit. At the end of a year, I was frustrated and confused because my daddy's clothes had always landed—wherever. But my husband hung up his coats, put his pants and shirts in the laundry basket, and knew exactly where he left his shoes.

Right away half of you hate me, because my husband is neat and your husband leaves a trail. Let me remind you that we all got married with a fifty-fifty chance of having either kind. To be fair, I'll add that he may know where his clothes are, but he can't find his glasses, never puts his shoe-shine kit away, and has forgotten to pay the phone bill a couple of times. Now, are we even?

The "Why-Didn't-I-Notice-That-Before!"

There are wonderful qualities in every spouse that only seem to surface after a few months of marriage. My brother-in-law, now a newlywed of one year, gave me the third degree over dinner one evening about my baby sister (his wife).

"Is she deaf or what?" he asked.

"What do you mean?" I replied calmly.

"Well, I'll be talking a blue streak, asking her questions, and she won't even hear me," he said. "And she will be sittin' right next to me. It drives me crazy! She just tunes me out. Whadaya think makes her do that? Does this run in your family?"

I will always love my husband for what he said next. NOTHING—ABSOLUTELY NOTHING. (For the moment.)

I gave my brother-in-law some helpful suggestions like, "Next time she tunes you out, try concentrating on how adorable and gorgeous she is, and the fact that she's also smart."

Ignoring me, he repeated, "Does this run in your family?"

I took one look at my little darlin' and knew that his self control was slipping. Out came what I'd been dreading all along.

"You learn ways of coping with this characteristic, ways of getting through," he said in a serious tone. "One night she was sitting around with one of those 'long-ago-and-far-far-away' faces, hearing only what she wanted. She never even noticed when I left the room. However, she did notice when I

15

re-entered the room, stark-naked, and sat down across the room to read a magazine. There are ways!"

My sister's marriage will never be the same!

DIFFERENCES BETWEEN MEN AND WOMEN

One of Us Is Odd

I had been married exactly two weeks, three and a half days, four hours and nine minutes. My apartment was cleaned to sparkling perfection, all 320 square feet of it. (This might be considered a large apartment in New York City, but in the South, it should have been a walk-in closet.) Nevertheless, it was my new home, and I had spent all day dusting where there was no dust and scrubbing the porcelain off the bathroom sink.

After scrubbing the grout between the bathroom floor tiles on my hands and knees with a toothbrush and Clorox, I sat back to revel in a brand-new sense of accomplishment, and I noticed that the skin on my knees was partially gone. At least the remaining skin was snowy white! I prayed that the skin would grow back by 4:30 when my husband arrived home.

It wasn't a pretty picture, but there I was. With my knees just shy of bleeding and with butterflies in my stomach, I waited for my husband to come home from work. I was absolutely positive he would be as excited about the clean grout as I was.

My hair was plumped and fluffy, my makeup freshly applied. I smelled and probably looked like one of the ladies who works behind the makeup counter of a large department store. (The ones who wear all the makeup they sell at one time.)

My husband came in, took me in his arms, and said, "How's my little babycakes?" The next words out of his mouth were, "You smell like Clorox and what's for dinner?" (He secretly feared that the two somehow went together.)

But I set him at ease by telling him what we were having: rice pudding with raisin and water chestnut casserole. He paused, followed by: "Sounds interesting." (Which I learned years later means, "This may be terminal, but I'll try to eat it anyway.")

His next stop was the bathroom. I stood in the hall, smiling a lot, just positive that at any moment he would fling open the bathroom door and say, "Wow, this bathroom sparkles like the sun and it smells so fresh! How did you ever do this in just one day? You must be exhausted!"

He eventually came out of the bathroom and said, "Sure smells like Clorox in there," as he walked into the dining room.

There you have it — a face-to-face confrontation with the differences between men and women. Men and women see things differently. I just knew he certainly was going to see the significance of sparkling, clean grout; and he was looking forward to something "less interesting" for dinner.

I no longer clean the bathroom, hoping for the approval of my husband. I have his approval and love. I clean for my own satisfaction and to live up to my own standards. Oh, about that meal — the rice pudding with raisin and water chestnut casserole — he sat down, ate, and smiled a lot, said "very interesting" three times (by now we know what that means), and I never made that dish again.

Nonetheless, this began my journey into gaining wisdom and understanding of the marriage relationship. Understanding means that you have gained the good sense not to make the same mistakes twice. Wisdom means the art of avoiding the mistakes in the first place. And learning to recognize and deal with the differences between men and women is the tricky part of the process.

Telephone — Friend or Foe

Shortly after learning that men and women have differing expectations, I soon learned that men and women don't view the telephone through the same lens either. A phone is a necessary evil that interrupts his thought processes and intrudes into his quiet moments at home. It's a means of conducting work, making deals, and conveying essential information.

The phone is basically the same tool for a woman. The difference comes in defining the term *essential information*.

The other night, my husband and I were sitting around enjoying a quiet evening at home (a rare occurrence now days; couples don't see each other often enough to grow tired of each other today). As I said, we were together when I remembered that I had to call Sara for lunch the next day. I picked up the phone and here's the conversation from my end.

"Sara, hi there! How are you?" (As if I hadn't seen her the day before.)

"Your balcony on your house did what? No!"

"What did you do with the dog?"

"Try bathing her in tomato juice."

"The fashion show was disastrous! The day you see me wearing those fashions will be the day after we all start going nude!"

"By the way, we need to set a time for lunch tomorrow to talk about the meeting next week. Could you meet me at 11:00? Okay, sounds good to me too. See you there."

I hung up the phone and found my husband staring at me, shaking his head.

"What?" I asked.

"That's absolutely incredible!" he said.

"What?" (I'm real good at asking just the right questions.)

"It took you five and a half minutes and four topics to get around to the reason you called her."

"Well, you can't just expect me to say, 'Lunch at 11:00 okay with you?'"

"Why not?" he said. "It covers everything you need to say."

From that, I could see that he didn't understand human relationships at all. Here's the same conversation from his perspective.

"Tom, this is Hank. Lunch tomorrow at 11:00 okay? Great. See you later." Click.

I hate to admit it—short, not too sweet, and definitely to the point.

My argument is that they could talk and never know whether the children are flunking algebra, the dog got sprayed by a skunk, or that the balcony just fell off the house. Important things like that.

It Makes a Big Difference Who Drives the Car

Our vows were still warm and the ink barely dry on the marriage license when I realized a fundamental difference between men and women that went beyond backpacking, bathroom grout, and telephones.

I will not become a back-seat driver. That's Back Seat with a capital "B." I've been known at a moment of weakness to open my mouth and make a few "suggestions" that I felt were in the best interests of our safety and well-being. Without exception, my suggestions have been soundly rejected, and it doesn't matter if we had just been picked up and blown over by an eighteen-wheeler. My husband assures me he has everything under control and I only imagined a narrow escape.

Once when I pushed the subject, he suggested that any minute he would pull over and let me drive. Who does he think he's kidding?

I drove to church one Sunday evening. It may sound unbelievable, but in just one and a half miles, he accused me of braking too slowly, tailgating, narrowly missing a light pole, and turning sharply. To hear him tell it, I'm lucky he didn't sue me for whiplash.

I pulled into the church parking lot, got out, and locked him in the car. (It's okay, he was smart enough to get out.)

Another car pulled in beside us and the wife hopped out from behind the wheel hurrying to catch up with me. The first words out of her mouth were, "You won't believe what that man said to me. He said, 'Woman, if I had to ride with you everyday, I'd die an early death!' "

"No!" I exclaimed. As we walked through the door, we glanced in the direction of our cars and both our husbands were still sitting inside. Recovering from shock, no doubt.

Differences Between Men and Women

Men and women are different, and most of you have noticed it. When you get married, you are put in the position of having to accept things that make absolutely no sense to you. If your husband has a forty-thousand-volume collection of books on the mating habits of the common gnat, you are supposed to let him build bookshelves in the living room to display them.

And you must do it. If you don't let him, years later you'll discover the reason he won't build you an art room out back is that you are being quietly punished for banishing his books. All the arguments in the world won't help. He won't see the significance of needing an entire wall for hanging a picture of your parents at their twenty-fifth wedding anniversary party.

Of course, your husband will also have to put up with your hobbies and interests. If you knit, it could take years, but he will eventually adjust to a wife who sits for hours talking to a pair of metal sticks with four million yards of yarn spread over her body.

If you sew — as in make your own clothes — you are a special category. Women who sew will drive 150 miles to buy a one-half yard of lace to finish a dress, all in the name of "saving money." Save yourself a lot of grief. Don't try to explain that one to your husband. Most of them don't shop, so they have no idea that you can't buy a dress for $14.95. And certainly, they are not prepared to handle the fact that a half-yard of lace alone can cost that much.

There are many of us who prefer shopping to sewing. In my case, if I want clothes on my body, shopping is my only hope.

A Penny Saved Is $15 Blown

Shopping is one of those words with the potential to raise the hair on a husband's neck. The day my husband comes home from a hard day at work and says, "Darlin', let's go to the mall — I feel a spending spree coming on," will be the day I'll know for sure he's walked over the edge and won't be back.

Just the other evening, my husband "agreed" to go shopping with me. (I didn't say he *never* went shopping.) This was one of those wonderful times when he was doing something just to please me, so off we went.

Somewhere between looking at blouses, trying on a new winter coat, and examining silver earrings, I realized he was no longer with me. I went searching for him and there he was — smack dab in the center of the store — sitting on a display, "posing" by the ugliest mannequin you've ever seen.

"What in the world are you doing?" No answer. "Come on," I said, "what do you think you're doing?"

"What in the world are you doing?" No answer. "Come on," I said, "what do you think you're doing?"

"Where's the shopping cart?" he asked.

"Shopping cart? Where do you think we are? Wal-Mart?" By that time, I couldn't remember why I wanted to go shopping in the first place. You can take a man shopping, but you can't make him pay attention.

On another shopping outing, he went into the book store — his favorite place — and hid from me in the photography section. Since that time, I am on to all of his tricks. Now that is the first place I look.

On another occasion I did have to call Mall security and report a missing husband, but I couldn't describe what he was wearing at the time of disappearance.

The second place I look for him now is in the cookie store. He's spent so much time there that they named a cookie after him. It comes in real handy. When I want to go to the Mall, I just start muttering under my breath, "Cookies, large, warm cookies. . ." It works every time! The way to the Mall *is* through a man's stomach.

There must be some men who enjoy shopping. All I can say is that I have yet to meet one. It may be that when I am traveling around the country performing and speaking after this book is released, some of you will come up to me and introduce your "shopping" spouses. You may try to tell me that he lives from spree to spree. But I'll tell you this: I won't believe a word of it.

When it comes to shopping, I have a gift my husband doesn't fully appreciate. I can sniff out a sale in bad weather, and like a bird dog pointing its prey, my car turns in the right direction.

Returning home from a recent successful expedition, I was loaded with packages. "What in the world have you bought?" he wanted to know.

"You won't believe it," I answered.

"Try me," he said with a slow grin that still drives me crazy after all these years.

"This was my lucky day. I bought eight sweaters and four of them cost a penny each," I told him as I dumped the sweaters on the bed. His face had one of those looks that said, "Okay, now give me the catch to this deal."

"It's a great deal. The other four were marked down to $12.99 each. Can you beat that?" I asked, feeling proud of myself. "I saved you $51.96."

"You know good and well that you hate lime green, and you wouldn't wear red to a dog fight," he muttered, as he turned to walk out of the room. "Yes, but . . ."

There's not even a remote possibility that I'm unique among my sex. I'm sure some of you are just like me. There's no telling how many of us there are, but I'm confident there are sufficient numbers to begin a "Shoppers Anonymous." We could have group therapy for people who purchase items they can't identify when they get home. There should be help for those of us who buy items we can't live without, and once they're hanging in our closet, can't quite figure out what to do with them. It takes me so long to put together an outfit that I've taken to keeping snack food in my closet to maintain my strength.

I witnessed a scene in a grocery store that may have been a turning point for me. There was a SALE cart filled to the rim with unlabeled canned goods. There were elbows flying in every direction as women scrapped to get as many of these unidentifiable cans as possible for fifteen cents each. I passed by feeling superior and grateful that I would never stoop to such a low—well, of course—if those had been end-of-the-season shoes . . .

I recently tried explaining to my husband that I needed a new pair of shoes. He walked into my closet and pointed an accusing finger. "Would you mind explaining to me what those are?" he asked.

"Don't be silly," I said. "They're shoes." When he started counting, I walked out of the closet and shut the door on him.

Fifteen minutes later, when he had a final count, he came looking for me. "Do you realize that there are twenty-six pairs of shoes in that closet?" he asked. He was sounding just a bit incredulous.

"You don't understand," I said. "Those shoes don't fit me." His mouth fell open so wide I could have stuffed half of Tennessee in it.

"That explains it then," he went on, "you're running a shoe sitting service for the ones Imelda Marcos was able to smuggle out."

Don't Fence Me In

I recently heard that there are women doing wardrobing for men. You know what wardrobing is: someone comes into the privacy of your home, enters your closet, and throws away half your clothes. After which, they leave you with a list of the season's latest designer items you can't live without, and a bill that you could live without.

Now, believe it or not, they are providing this service to our husbands—make that to somebody's husband. I could imagine what my husband's closet would look like after a wardrobe consultant finished with it. Empty. Stripped down to bare walls. It's as likely as a blizzard in July for my husband to allow anyone to touch his wardrobe. There are items in his possession that he considers sacred. I fully expect him to have his Ralph Lauren safari jacket bronzed when it's finally in tatters. I'm quite sure he will hang it on the wall in his studio beside other career memorabilia.

One wintry morning I stood at the door to kiss him goodbye. It was twenty degrees outside with a wind chill of frostbite proportions. As he passed by in his denim jeans, cotton shirt, sweater, and Ralph Lauren safari jacket, I said,

"Don't you think it would be a good idea to wear your wool coat today?"

Without missing a step, he grinned and said, "That coat's too confining. I save it for 'cold' days."

We were leaving for an evening out recently, and he walked in wearing—you guessed it—the famous jacket. "You're NOT wearing THAT to dinner, are you?"

"What's wrong with this?" he said.

"That coat was alive before 'I Love Lucy' reruns. And you might as well carry a sign 'This Coat Has Been in Mothballs for Forty Years.'"

"Well," he said as he headed for the door, still wearing the coat, "if it's THAT old, I'll just wear a sign that says, 'This Coat Saw Moses Part the Red Sea,' and I'll be the hit of the party."

You can't win with a guy like that and, for once, he had the last word. You also can't manipulate a guy like that, and I'm glad. Any day now, I'm going to quit trying.

This is a man who began his career in television news and is now a commercial photographer. He hangs out of helicopters to get the perfect shot of a truck pulling into a truck stop. He has photographed the famous, the infamous, and the tedious. He has photographed the Shah of Iran, John F. Kennedy, and Lyndon B. Johnson. And all of this while wearing some version of the outfit previously described. He has his own brand of class.

He buys quality and keeps it till it dies a slow death. Then we, the family, are asked to mourn the passing of a cherished item. Then begins the search for another "whatever it was."

I have to admit that I wasted considerable energy trying to reform and transform my husband's attire. This temptation seems so contradictory, considering one of the things I admired about him when we met was his casual manner, his unique style. His style suited his career and lifestyle, and no one ever looked better in jeans and a wool blazer than he.

But shortly after we married, a sort of insanity hit me. I began to try to see him the way I imagined other people perceived him. I worried about what they might think of a grown man who wore jeans to church. I worried that they wouldn't like him or take the time to get to know him if he were different. We had more than a few discussions about this subject, which often resulted in both of us leaving for church in separate cars.

Somewhere between standing breathless at the altar and the seven-year-itch, we discovered something: the very differences that so attracted us in the first place became the very qualities we started to attack and attempted to change in each other.

I can save you a lot of anxiety and harsh words. Let each other be who you are. Let your husband be what he is and never create a mental picture of what you *think* he should be. It will never work. The pressure created by trying to impose our wills on another person is destructive and a complete waste of time. I had the good sense to fall in love with my husband the way he was, and finally, the good sense to want him to stay that way.

Which brings me to the most important word when it comes to our differences: acceptance. Both husbands and wives come preassembled with no instructions about how to correct major flaws in the manufacturing. People want to "correct" everything about each other, according to their own preconceived notions of a perfect spouse. It just doesn't work that way. Strong marriages are built when we spend less time correcting and more time accepting.

I accept the fact that my husband talks less than I do. He thinks for what seems to be hours before he speaks (and rarely has to apologize for what he says). This quality used to make my face twitch. Now, not only do I accept it, I appreciate it. (Now, I have a simple eye twitch.)

He accepts a lot of my traits, which to some husbands would become a source of irritation. I'm a social butterfly and like to meet everyone in a crowded room. But I like him to stay right by my side while I do it.

I buy shoes that don't fit and clothes that don't match, and a thousand other things he could use against me. He accepts me, flaws and all. Acceptance for us began in our hearts, and continues with a conscious effort in our minds to take delight in each other. (Unfortunately that includes our differences.)

My husband and I recently moved to a new house, and during the first week, I managed to lock my car in the garage, along with the three garage door openers, while locking myself out of the house at the same time (which must run in my family as you will see later on). I try to make something worthwhile of every crisis, which isn't a bad philosophy of life since I spend so much time in the middle of one. So, not having met my next door neighbor, and needing to use her phone to call my husband (better known as the rescue squad), I walked next door and introduced myself, "I've locked my keys in the house, and my car in the garage, and I need to use your phone." This makes a pretty good first impression as to the kind of person they now having living next door. She seemed delighted that I had locked myself out — or rather she seemed delighted to meet me — and graciously offered to drive me to wherever my husband was so I could pick up his keys. We began an easy and immediate friendship, which proved her to be open minded and willing to give even an idiot a chance.

My neighbors are a long-time married couple. He's eighty years old; she's seventy-seven. They are both still young, active, and very much bending and flexing, as marriage is known to require.

Over coffee one morning, she said, "You know, if I had given up all my friends when we married, we would really have no friends." He is somewhat of a loner and now retired from a career in television electronics. Socially, he is content with quiet evenings at home. She also had a career, and through the years has maintained healthy friendships with other women. I thought, *Fifty years of marriage and they still remain a round peg married to a triangular peg living with, and in spite of, differences, the likes of which have sent many young couples seeking the "perfect mate."*

PROLOGUE TO COMMUNICATION
Non-Verbal Responses

*T*hat oldest child of yours may be the one to watch. I know, I'm the oldest child.

When I was fourteen, I discovered the ultimate revenge on my mother and daddy for using me for child-rearing practice. I prayed for a baby sister and got one.

Never once did I consider the age statistics: the fact that my mother was thirty-eight and my daddy, forty-two, when she was born. Nor did I compute ahead to discover that when this same baby graduated from college, my daddy would be making decisions about where to retire and filling out paperwork for a pension.

I did think they needed someone to keep them young in their golden years. Someone who would prove to them that the "older" daughter wasn't nearly so difficult by comparison. At two weeks of age, when our little bundle cried at night, I jumped up to feed her. (That was when bottle feeding was "in.") And I guess Momma figured that feeding her was the *least* I could do!

That night after feeding her, that baby looked right at me and said, "Sissie, I want to sleep with you tonight." And she slept with me until I left for college several years later. To say we were attached to each other would be a classic understatement.

So, years later when Momma and Daddy said things like, "She's going to be the death of me," and "I'll never live through getting this one raised," I just shrugged my shoulders and said: "Oh, you'll survive. She's just keeping you flexible." Then Daddy's face would take on the look of a rabid dog, and I would excuse myself and head for home.

Now that twenty-five-year-old baby sister is a newlywed. Her wedding was perfect. She had the kind of radiance a bride should have. I was the matron of honor, and yes, I cried. I cried because she was so beautiful. I cried because she was happy. I cried because I was happy. I cried because she kept telling me how happy she was, and because if she said it one more time, I would be a very sick person. I cried because she was leaving as soon as the wedding was over — not exactly because she was leaving but because she, rather, "they" were leaving for ten days in Hawaii for their honeymoon.

I cried actually because I could still remember my honeymoon. Just thinking about it made a chill run down my spine, over my hips, and across my shoulders, a feeling similar to that of touching an electric fence.

My sister's reception was to have been outdoors. It would have been lovely. Ferns had been delivered, lattice work set in place, wrought iron chairs put in place: a lovely setting for an outdoor wedding reception except for one factor — the unrelenting rain that persisted throughout the day.

I kept hunting down our dad to see if he was building another ark, but he was stumbling around the church with a dazed look on his face.

The reception was moved inside to the church's small reception room. No lattice work. No wrought iron chairs. No outdoors. But the bride was totally unaffected by the rain—she was happy. She kept saying nothing in the world would upset her on this most wonderful day. Then she remembered the garter and asked me to find the groom and get it.

I located the groom's father and asked him to fetch the garter. The groom's father returned, looking slightly grim. His son had forgotten to buy one.

I said, "No problem! She's so laid back, I don't think anything could upset her. I'll just tell her there's no garter."

She was combing out her hair by this time, fully dressed in her scrumptious wedding gown and its forty trillion seed pearls hand-sewn by our mother. She was smiling at no one and humming to herself.

"There is no garter."

"What?"

"There is no garter. You husband-to-be forgot to buy one."

She was no longer smiling, and her humming came to an abrupt halt. Being her older sister and wiser than she, I remained "upbeat" and positive about the whole thing (after all, it's just a garter).

"It's no problem, is it? It's just a tradition. You said nothing could make you unhappy on this particular day, you being so happy and all"—her look of panic could have wilted all the gladiolus at the reception.

As I've said before, I'm real perceptive. She was *not* going to be happy without a $6.95 garter. I walked out of the dressing room and found the father of the groom waiting patiently with a look that said, "How far is it to the nearest department store?"

He dispatched a devoted friend to go to the four corners of the earth and find a garter. Thirty minutes later, and not one minute too soon, we had a garter, a happy bride, and a groom who narrowly escaped being in hot water.

You can see from this story how little of what we say really means what we say. It is the "look" we give each other that really counts. There were non-verbals going back and forth faster than a tennis ball at Wimbledon. The amazing part was that those of us who intercepted the looks acted on them with hardly a word spoken.

This must prove the saying: "It is not what you say, it's what you do that matters most."

FOUR

SILENCE ISN'T
GOLDEN

Communication

$\mathcal{C}$ommunication ought to be simple. After all, this is America. Most of us speak English. I don't know how far you have to drive in any one direction to find someone who speaks *and* understands English, but I would guess it would be more than a few miles.

English is not an easy language to speak, and it continues to become more and more complicated. The word *finesse* once meant the delicacy of performance, or skillful handling of a situation, an excellent quality for spouses to have.

Today *finesse* is also a shampoo.

Without words, life would be so quiet, so peaceful, so . . . nothing. There are forty trillion words with which to communicate. As adolescents we don't speak normal English, and not too many years later, many of us find ourselves married. We then discover that not only is our choice of words important, but also that the emotion and inflection we use can pack a big wallop. We learn in kindergarten that words can be used to accomplish manipulation. But even before kindergarten, we learn all we need to know about several communication skills. Ever heard a non-verbal infant after a sibling takes away a toy?

The Drip Who Trips Over His Pouting Lips

It is not too difficult to believe that there are children who have perfected pouting to get their way. It may be surprising, though, to learn that some of these same children enjoy the results so much they maintain a healthy repertoire of pouting routines and carry them right into marriage.

For the sake of those who have never seen pouting and have never tried pouting, let me elaborate. Something happens that displeases a person. This person is displeased, upset, and even angry that things are not going his or her way. Rather than work toward a solution in a sensible way by communicating with words, he or she POUTS.

P-O-U-T. To pout. Although it may sound like a bad case of gas, Webster defines it as follows: *"Pout. A verb. To express disapproval or resentment by protruding the lips to look sulky or sullen."*

This is the act an eight-year-old can turn on that has a profound effect on the parent who witnesses it. A simple question such as, "May I have an ice cream sandwich?" and a simple answer, such as, "No, you just had one and may not have another," can have interesting results. At this point, the child doesn't give up. That would be throwing in the towel too fast.

Next, the big beg. "Oh, Mommy, please just ONE more?" "The answer is no. I said no, I mean no. NO. Period. Do you speak English? . . . N-O!"

Before the last no is out of Mommy's mouth, the lips are already having a spasm and are leaving the child's face, headed in the general direction of the floor. The eyes have filled with tears and no wipers are available. Large tears threaten to spill over those long lashes, between upward glances to see if you catch the FULL effect. She's trying to squeeze those tears out onto rosy cheeks, at which point you will undoubtedly break down, and her mission will be accomplished.

In the next scene, she is walking away with an ice cream sandwich, and you have just been outmaneuvered by an eight-year-old. This proves P. T. Barnum's theory that a sucker is born every minute.

Pouting in a female child is the stuff that turns a father's heart into putty. Pouting makes a mother wish the child's father had signed up for the Foreign Legion *before* she met him!

The best advice I can give you is: the next time your child pouts, wet her lips and stick her to the refrigerator.

Pouting knows no boundaries, and this same technique appears in many marriages. Adults carry this to an all-time low when they use it against their spouses. Adult-type pouting has less emphasis on the begging and more emphasis on the "sullenness," which is just another word for someone "puffed up" who refuses to talk.

The first time he hurt my feelings — the day after the honeymoon — I put on my best pout. After I had pouted fifteen consecutive minutes, he uttered not one single word! Next I pulled out another childhood trick: the I'll-take-my-toys-and-leave method. I left the room. He followed me into our bedroom and said, "I think this is yours."

Curiosity always gets the better of me. "What?" I asked.

"Your bottom lip," he answered. "It fell off and the dog thought it was a new frisbee."

After I finished laughing, I couldn't remember why I was pouting in the first place. Pouting in a marriage reduces one person to a child and forces the other spouse to become the parent. It is difficult to tell which person is the most miserable.

Melodrama

Sometime after kindergarten we learn that if pouting works, then melodrama must be even better. When a young child flings himself or herself on a bed, or dissolves in a puddle of tears in the middle of the supermarket because you won't let them buy a tweny-pound Hershey bar, you can rest assured that they have discovered the technique of melodrama.

Melodrama is another negative communication skill that should fall to the wayside as we mature. If it were to completely disappear, half the marriage counselors in the world would be out of a job.

Melodrama, when used by an adult, takes on a much more serious vein than it does in childhood. There are millions of women and men who have perfected it to such a degree that their spouses think melodrama is perfectly normal behavior. They never realize that a home without constant crises and bad overacting is even possible — much less desirable.

I have drawn some conclusions from watching families with young children. Some children are more prone to melodrama than others, but all of them are capable of it.

And parents tolerate melodrama and manipulation. Those parents go around looking like they have been run over by a Mack truck. Other parents are not fooled for one minute and are inclined to walk off without paying admission to the show. *Sometimes* when children notice that there is no audience, there will be no performance.

I have NEVER used melodrama on my husband. Well, once, just once. We had a "will-to-will" collision, and I threatened to commit suicide with the cutting edge of the Saran-wrap box. He looked at me the same way our labrador retriever does when her ears perk up a bit and she cocks her head to one side, as if to say, "You got to be kidding." Then he shook his head, walked out the front door, and went to work.

The Fine Art of Tap-Dancing
Through the Backdoor

What it was, was a TV movie. Actually, it was a TV movie he didn't want to watch. So, what he used on me was what I call the backdoor technique of communication.

It goes like this. He says to me, "Are you sure you want to watch this?"

P-A-U-S-E.

Meanwhile, I'm thinking, *Now why is he asking me if I'm sure I want to watch this movie. I'm sitting here, aren't I? Watching it, aren't I?* "Why? Don't you want to watch it?" I reply.

No response.

Several minutes pass before he asks again, "Do you *really* want to watch this movie?"

This time I admit to being more than slightly irritated and say, "Well, obviously you don't want to watch it because every two and a half minutes you offer me another opportunity *not* to watch it." Growing tired of the game, I respond in a voice that shows my irritation. "If you don't want to watch the movie, why don't you just *say so?*"

"I didn't say I didn't want to watch it, and I don't appreciate your tone of voice," he replies in a huff as he gets up from the sofa.

Suddenly, I'm overcome with brilliance in the art of communication. I say, "You're acting stupid and immature; do you want to watch this movie or not? You're being irrational too!"

"THAT does it!" he says. After years of marriage I have learned what THAT means. THAT means, "Now I'm going to show you some real maturity," which he does by leaving the room. This is what I call the "I'll-take-my-toys-and-leave" method.

I'm real slow, but by now I get the picture. He doesn't want to watch this movie.

Scenes like this make me wonder whether we ever truly acquire adult ways of communicating. In the best of times we do, but because the intimacy of marriage creates a desire for shared experiences between two different personalities, we have all the ingredients for occasional fireworks.

It's easy to see the previous situation the way it should have been. The husband: "I don't want to watch this movie. I think I'll watch something in the other room." But he had a desire for a shared experience, and I was not cooperating with the beautiful opportunity he gave me.

The Solution

While he was still out of the room I switched the channel. Lo and behold, a submarine movie was playing. Just what I wanted to see!

"Come in here," I said. "This looks interesting." (By now we know what "interesting" means!) He came in; I worked on my writing; he watched the submarine movie.

My above technique is what I call zigging and zagging. Sometimes I zig, which pleases him. Sometimes he zags, which pleases me.

Now, there will be certain groups of people who will say that he manipulated me, that I didn't stand up for my rights. But while certain people prefer to keep score and count their causes, I am working on a wonderful marriage.

The 'Ole "Heel-and-Toe" Routine

There are adults—yes, married adults—who spend their lives tap-dancing all around the true subject. Tap-dancing is a perfect description of this type of communication. If you have watched a real tap dancer, their feet touch the floor with the toe first and then the heel. They move around a lot, skipping all over the floor, with unusual moves. It's difficult to follow a good dancer's feet, they move so fast.

This pretty well describes those of us who are never willing to come right out and say what we really feel. We develop some pretty good moves for drawing attention away from the heart of the matter. It's difficult to have a good argument with a tap dancer; he or she keeps changing the subject on you. If you are a tap-dancing communicator, chances are that when a spouse or a friend zeroes in on exactly what's bothering you, you deny it—The Great Mystery Move.

Many of you are the *victims* of a tap-dancing spouse and many of you *are* the tap-dancing spouse. For those of you who have polished your heel-and-toe routine up to this point in your life, I suggest the following: scratch the routine. Box it up. Put the tap shoes away. Ask yourself why you avoid saying exactly what's on your mind in the first place. Are you secretly wishing you had married a mind reader, and you continue attempting to turn him or her into one? Then you blame him or her for not being one and say things like, "You can't see the nose in front of your face." You keep on sending out clues, but he doesn't understand the rules and probably doesn't want to play the game.

Some of our spouses may be perfectly willing to learn how to say what's on their minds when we prove to them they can do so without condemnation or ridicule or even an argument.

It has taken me years and a couple of wrinkles to teach my husband to accept my feelings. There have been too many conversations that went like this: "Now, if you would just listen to me. That's the problem with you. You never listen!"

It took me far too long to rewrite that opening line. Now it goes like this: "Darlin', I want to share something with you that is really important to me."

He says, "Okay, what is it?" Now, when he says, "What is it?", I've learned to approach things from a more positive angle without dumping on him with both barrels. A major breakthrough came when I learned that he responds differently to a more controlled tone in my voice. If I border on sounding out-of-control, he starts backpedaling right out of the conversation. And sometimes right out of the house. Or worse, we end up in a shouting match in which there are no winners.

Finally learning to control my tongue, I've been amazed at the results. I've learned to speak slowly and more thoughtfully when dealing with a sensitive subject. My husband is much less defensive now. He listens to my feelings and needs without reacting in anger. In short, we have learned the truth in that age-old, Dale Carnegie principle: "To win an argument, even when you may be right, is to lose a friend." And my husband is one friend I can't afford to lose. Too many adults remain in the adult version of the "terrible twos" syndrome: me, my, and mine. "I'm me. I matter more than you. My needs are everything."

"Pearl in a Pigsty"

Occasionally, there is a rare piece of wisdom on television. It's like finding a pearl in a pigsty, but it does happen.

Two women surgeons were talking on a program—a young, budding surgeon and an older, wiser surgeon. The young woman surgeon was parading her authority like a peacock who had just discovered its plumes. As a result, she was alienating all of her male coworkers. Beyond that, she was taking unnecessary risks with her new-found authority just to prove something.

She finally said to the older female surgeon, "It's tough. How do you find the balance?" The wiser surgeon said quietly, "I am a highly trained, highly skilled surgeon. I am quick and sure with a scalpel. But every Thanksgiving, without fail, my husband carves the turkey."

Jesus said, "He who would make himself least on earth will be the greatest in heaven."

It could change our marriages to live by this bit of wisdom: "Never 'demand' justice and mercy from our spouses, but *never* cease to give it."

Wisdom Is a Cultured Pearl, and If
I Live Long Enough, I May Get One

My mother-in-law once told me that when my husband was growing up, the quickest way to get him not to do something was to *demand* that he do it. "Well, well," I said, "some things never change!"

The wiser I get, the older I am. Or is it the other way around? I'm old enough to see the truth that most of us don't respond positively to demands. Demanding a particular response or behavior from our partners usually stirs up World War III. In *our* house, it's the equivalent to sticking one's head in a hornet's nest.

As the old saying goes, I may be ugly but I ain't stupid! I'm learning not to demand certain things from my husband. As I try to give what I know pleases him, a funny thing has happened: he has begun to do some of the things I used to demand.

So, there we have another truth. It may be that all things come to those who *don't* ask or demand it, but who *do* it themselves. If that sounds familiar, it's because it is. It's called the Golden Rule: Do unto others (and that includes spouses) as you would have them . . .

If your goal is to *win* an argument or have *all* your needs met at any cost, you're probably living in a lot of turmoil. You probably have a spouse carrying around an oversized load of resentment as well. You may be winning the battle, but losing at having a satisfying marriage.

We teach our children to give and take with playmates. We teach them to share their toys. Then we approach our marriages with an attitude of selfishness that would cause a two-year-old to blush. Couples fight over everything from who left the empty shampoo bottle in the bathtub to what the dog's food is doing in the kitchen sink. We grow past the terrible twos when we finally identify those areas where we are wasting valuable time and depleting much needed energy on trivial pursuits.

Black Hole of Calcutta

Some of my thoughts are born in the Black Hole of Calcutta, and I wish they would die there. The tongue can soothe a crying child, sympathize with a neighbor, and then turn around and slash a spouse to the quick. Yes, I admit. I, too, have done it.

On at least one occasion, my husband made a lasting impression on me. He asked if I would like to see his wounds and began to unbutton his shirt. He made me laugh, but also made me realize that wounds from words do leave injuries. They go deep within a person and can crush the human spirit.

How many of us remember cutting words that were said to us in high school? Chances are we vividly remember what the person said to us as well as the emotion with which it was delivered.

When I was in the eighth grade, someone told me I had a nose like Danny Thomas. I believed him and have only in the past two years accepted my nose. (Now you can't wait to check out this nose.)

Picking, Poking, and Prodding

We use words to pick at our spouses when we're agitated with them. We poke them with words when we're angry, and we prod them when they don't do things the way we want. Whether it's picking, poking, or prodding—when done to a spouse — negative words amount to a criminal offense and are punishable by waking up one morning in a king-sized bed alone.

I've been a captive audience, along with other guests, at dinner parties where a conversation between a husband and wife became verbal combat. He begins telling a story, but seconds into it, the wife gives in to the urge to interrupt. She has had the urge since the moment he opened his mouth. Her face became scrunched up and her lips began to move. So, she prods him with all of the details of the story he's not getting right. After which, he gives her a funny look and continues with the story. Realizing that her husband has totally ignored her first prodding, this gal comes at it with the persistence of a woodpecker trying to penetrate a tin roof.

"Why can't you tell anything the way it happened? It was such-and-such, not so-and-so."

After a pause so pregnant that quintuplets could have been born, the poor husband's eyes begin to bulge out of his head, and he responds a bit louder than he should, "Have you lost your mind? It most certainly *was* such-and-such and, furthermore, it was *not* so-and-so."

She will not be outdone. "I beg your pardon. You never remember *anything* the way it happened, and yes, I must have lost my mind. I married you, didn't I?"

Couples who do this to each other should have their communication restricted to blinking once for yes, twice for no!

After going through a painfully uncomfortable experience listening to the picking, poking, and prodding of another couple on one occasion, I grabbed my husband's arm, pulled him to the car, and shoved a safety pin and blank piece of paper into his hand.

"Stick your finger and sign in blood that even if I take leave of my senses and tell a story that is complete fiction, you will never treat me that way. And furthermore, I solemnly promise never to pick, poke, and prod, even if you tell a story with all of the facts completely rearranged, which, by the way, you often do. Did you know that the other night at . . ." (I've never been threatened with a safety pin before, but it didn't take long for me to get the point.)

A married couple can take vacations together for fifty years, rear a half-dozen children, and they will never recall exactly the same details of anything they've ever done.

After listening carefully to my parents, I've concluded that they lived separate lives together because of the phenomenon just mentioned. None of their recollections coincide. Neither one will give an inch and each of them is *right*. This only leads me to assume that one of the long-term hazards of marriage is loss of memory, or else we all become a bunch of liars.

When you are a newlywed, you should begin a practice that will avoid numerous arguments over the next twenty to thirty years. Write down everything that happens to the two of you. Both of you must sign it and have it notarized. This will become the only truthful version of your life you'll ever use.

The only alternative to the notarized version of your life is for one of you to keep your mouth firmly closed when the other is talking. This is definitely the most difficult method, but it is guaranteed to impress your friends and endear you to your spouse, and believe me, it is better to impress your friends than to shock them.

I didn't get married to have a partner with whom to engage in either verbal or physical combat. If I had wanted that, I would have joined the Army. But sometimes, even with the best of intentions, arguments do happen.

Silence Isn't Golden, Slamming Doors Is . . .

Next time you are in the mood for a real zinger of an argument, I recommend doing it over the telephone. This method has several advantages, not the least of which is that you don't have to look at each other. Not looking at each other is a plus, because you can't see the "encouraging" expressions each of you sends the other.

Probably the best advantage is that when words become too heated, you have several options. One being, you simply put the phone back on the hook. This is known to some as hanging up and would probably *not* be recommended by James Dobson. Though, if the truth be told, he's probably tried it! This technique for arguing lets you know immediately if your little darlin' is sincerely upset or just arguing to perfect his skills.

If he is serious, the phone will ring in approximately seven and a half seconds. At which time, you have the opportunity to exercise one of the better options. DON'T ANSWER IT. The distinct benefit of this approach is that unless he works close enough to home, hops in his car, and shows up in your living room, this argument is virtually over.

The desired outcome of hanging up is that by the time he *does* come home that evening, both of you — depending on your emotional age — will have had time to simmer down, and maybe even *forget about it*. But remember: newlyweds *never* forget anything; thirty-to-forty-year-olds will remember an argument, but won't recall exactly what it was about; forty-to-fifty-year-olds won't remember who hung up on whom; fifty-to-sixty-year-olds won't remember talking to each other that day.

The fact is, if you're the sort of person who wants absolute resolution to each and every argument, *none of these techniques will bring you any satisfaction*. Because those who are driven to resolve everything beyond a shadow of a doubt are usually the bring-it-up-and-stomp-all-over-it sort. They will keep on doing just that — bringing it up and stomping on it — whether the spouse enjoys it or not.

We dredge up bad topics for several reasons. We may be holding a grudge and want to be sure no one forgets. We may feel that a satisfactory solution has not been found, so we pick at it, hoping a solution will materialize from hashing it out one more time. Some of us persist in bringing up an old subject because we think we're right and won't give up until someone agrees with us.

This is a form of marital torture and accomplishes nothing except in the mind of the perpetrator. I've decided that people who are this bring-it-up-and-stomp-all-over-it type are not actually to blame for this trait. They learned it from their parents.

"The Wife No One Deserves"

The names have been changed in this story to protect the guilty.

The scene: Movie theater lobby.

"Oh, look darlin', there's Nimrod and Fluffo." (Apologies to anyone who might happen to be named Nimrod or Fluffo, but if I'm ever in your town I'd like to see you with my own two eyes.)

Next scene: The two couples approach each other.

"Nimrod," my husband begins, "it's been a long time. How are you?"

Nimrod open his mouth to speak but just before producing a single syllable, his dearly devoted wife, Fluffo, answers for him.

"We've been just fine, busy . . . real busy . . . my, it's been a long time . . . when was the last time we saw you all?" (She doesn't even pause to suck air.) ". . . Saw your son, he's really growing up . . . my, my . . . it's been a while . . . I was just sayin' to so-and-so the other day that such-and-such and blah-blah-blah-blah-blah!. . ."

Nimrod seems to be shrinking a bit. I think to myself that the ultrasonic vibrations of Fluffo's vocal chords have caused all the disks between his vertebrae to collapse. The drone of her voice continues in the background telling us more than we want to know. Finally, this woman pauses to gasp for air. During the temporary break in this nondialogue, my husband attempts to pull dear Nimrod back into the conversation with "tell me, are you still selling fossils to museums?"

Very pointedly I focus my eyes on the husband and eagerly await his response. It looks hopeful. He musters a bit of self-esteem, straightens his shoulders, and open his mouth to speak. We smile encouragingly and just when it seems we will have his answer—you guessed it! Fluffo rushes in, and poor, dear, Nimrod steps into oblivion behind this woman whose tongue runs in high gear and rarely makes a pit stop.

We finally excuse ourselves and when we are well out of earshot I say, "What do you think about when you're around women who talk too much?"

"Homicide," he answers.

"Do you think this poor guy lost his ability to speak for himself before he married her or afterward?"

"I'd vote for the latter," he responds.

There Must Be Something to Learn From All of This

After the second or third or maybe even the seventh year of marriage, you begin to wonder why no one ever told you that marriage requires so much *work*—and not mopping the floor kind of work either. Our parents didn't tell us because they were afraid we would never leave home. I also have my suspicions that they didn't tell us because they haven't quite figured it out for themselves.

Good marriages are hard work.

But good marriages are *worth* the hard work. Good marriages are a shared effort. Good marriages require communication. Good marriages do not just happen as if by magic. First, they are desired, then committed to, then worked on—*forever and ever.*

Marriage could be eternal bliss if someone could find a cure for the "common tongue." Our tongues should have a beeper connected to the brain. A beeper like this could spare us a lot of marital disasters by warning us *before* the wrong words come out.

If you have ever tried to take back words after they have been spoken, you quickly learn that it cannot be done. The only thing to do then is clean up the mess, which takes longer than it took for the words to come out of your mouth in the first place. You try apologizing: "I'm so sorry. Please forgive me. I didn't mean that." Then your spouse says, "If you didn't mean it, why did you say it," and for that, there is no answer.

In Edith Schaeffer's book *The Tapestry*, she makes the comparison between our relationships and a beautifully woven tapestry. Ill-spoken words are a tear in the tapestry. The tear can be repaired, but the patch-up job will always be visible upon close inspection.

I believe that unhealthy patterns like this can be broken and replaced by healthy ones. Perhaps looking at the way we communicate will help us identify the problems that are killing what marriage is meant to be. Happiness can be a matter of choosing to walk through a door marked, "I don't want to be this way any more."

FIVE

FAMOUS LINES FROM EVERY MARRIAGE
Questions and Confusions

*A*fter you've been married a few years, there are certain words that can curdle your buttermilk. You know what they are in your own marriage, and chances are, many of the famous lines are the same everywhere.

I learned some of mine from my mother and daddy. This one is a particular favorite: "Have you seen my keys?" This one is always on the tip of my daddy's tongue. I figured it up once and in forty-three years of marriage, my daddy has spent twenty-seven years, three and a half months looking for his keys.

I made brilliant suggestions that would eliminate the problem such as, "Put a hook beside the back door and put the keys on it every time you come into the house."

He agreed that was a good idea and then went right on losing his keys. I love it! We were discussing this as a family one evening and my daddy came out with what is now a famous line in our family: "I've spent half my life locked out of the house."

Now you would think that after forty-some years of marriage, he would have earned his own house key and that it would be on the ring with his car keys. Nooooo. That's too easy. It would take all the mystery out of life. I've decided that the key business is a game Momma and Daddy like to play. Momma and I can go shopping, be out for about three hours, when she suddenly remembers Daddy.

"I bet James is home and can't get into the house," she says.

"Well, it's his own fault," I say. "He can just 'putter' until we get home" (which makes me sound hardhearted).

But the next thing I know, Momma is muttering something about Daddy being out in the garden in his best suit because he can't get into the house, and I turn my car toward home. We pull into the driveway and there he is, out in the garden wearing his best Sunday suit, picking beans. That's when I remember the line, "I've spent half my life locked out of the house," and decide that "half his life" is too conservative an estimate.

There was the time when he was locked out on a midwinter day with the temperature holding steady at twenty degrees. He decided to go down to the woods and cut a dead limb off of a tree. He did a real good job, too. It fell on his head and cut a gash about an inch and a half long.

When my sister came home, a forlorn voice called out to her from the metal shed behind the house, "Miriam, I'm in here." She opened the shed door, and there he was, piled up on some hay in his Sunday suit with blood all over him.

"Daddy! What in the world are you doing in here?" she asked, dealing with first things first. "I am locked out of the house," he said, sounding real pitiful.

"Daddy, did you know there's blood all over your head?" She's a nurse first and a humanitarian second.

After this incident, I suggested he have the house key surgically attached to his right hand.

After growing up in a family like this, I was well prepared for the chaos of marriage. What I was not prepared for was a husband who always knows where his keys are. I had already screwed hooks by all of the doors in the house, and they've never been used.

Have You Seen My Socks?

What I was *not* prepared for was keeping up with 321 pairs of socks that never match. So another famous line is, "Have you seen my socks?" Like they're starring in their own Broadway show.

"Yeah, the last time I saw them, they were making a right turn at 11th and West Main, heading for the Donut Den." He then gives me one of those looks and sticks his head deeper into his sock drawer.

I found the perfect solution to this problem when I had been married six months. I carefully matched each pair of socks, then sewed the toes together. He woke me at 6:00 A.M. the next morning to tell me his socks had grown together in the drawer. It had seemed like a good idea at the time. But to tell you the truth, as he stood there wearing only his socks with his toes connected, I had to admit, "Honey, you just don't look right to me."

I did not get married to keep up with someone else's socks. But it wasn't long before I realized that, yes indeed, it *was* my responsibility — and everyone in the family knew it but me. The second a pair of socks turns up missing from action or mismatched, I'm the one who's interrogated.

Socks have a mind of their own. They take permanent vacations while in the washing machine.

Our son's socks are in a category of their own. I admire every mother who rears more than one son and still has sense of smell that hasn't permanently shut down from abuse. That boy of ours sweats glue. I'm sure of it because his socks walk around the house on their own. I caught a pair headed into the laundry room one evening. They took a left, went straight to the washing machine, took a giant leap, and committed sockacide. I am trying to convince his father to build a compartment on the outside of our house for dirty socks and tennis shoes, and he is close to giving in.

"This Will Only Take a Minute"

Somewhere just behind "Where are my keys?" and "Have you seen my socks?" come these famous lines: "It'll only take a minute" and "I'll be right back." Never believe a father or a husband when these words come out of his mouth. I learned this when I was only ten years old.

Those were the words Daddy said to Momma as he closed the car door. We were sitting in the car outside a funeral home (my dad is a preacher). This was not a new experience for us, and we were well acquainted with ways to entertain ourselves in a car over long periods of time.

On this occasion, Daddy was right for a change. It took only about thirty-two seconds. My brother Jim and I were practicing gymnastics in the backseat when he went flying out the car window and landed on his head on the curb. That was the quickest visit to a funeral home that my daddy every made, interrupted by an unscheduled stop in the emergency room to get stitches. To this day, my brother says that it was my fault. I say it was because we had been to one funeral home too many.

"I'll Be Right Back"

I don't trust anyone who says, "I'll be right back," and with good reason! When I was growing up, we had a cherished family pet. He was a prize coon hound. And somewhere along the way, we were given a goat. We were real creative and named him Billy the Goat. When we finally gave up trying to domesticate Billy to city life, we decided to return him to my granddad's farm in Murfreesboro, Tennessee.

One warm summer day, we loaded the car with all of our luggage, three children, Momma and Daddy, Jug (the prize coon hound who went everywhere we did), and Billy the Goat. All the luggage rode in the back seat with us because Jug and Billy were in the trunk of the car. (I was twenty-one before I learned that the trunk of a car is for luggage.)

Now Daddy could never pass through a town without going by to see someone he knew. It's a malady that afflicts preachers and small town doctors! The words, "I'll be right back," were our first clue that we were in for sitting a good long spell.

On this particular day, Daddy and Momma stopped in downtown Murfreesboro and went into one of the local stores, saying as they left us in the car, "We'll be right back." They had no sooner disappeared from sight when things began to happen.

The rear end of Daddy's car took on a life of its own. Sounds of a very irritated coon hound and a definitely disturbed goat began to emanate from the trunk. There was bleating the likes of which I've never heard since and growling that would stand on end the hair on a grizzly bear.

Then the car began to move up and down, back and forth, up and down. The noise level continued to rise. I looked around and found my two brave brothers on the floor of the back seat. I sat in the front and acted as if all of this was perfectly normal behavior for a red '57 Chevy. This may be the moment I entered show business. I smiled and bobbed my head up and down, and smiled some more at the people who passed by. Actually, no one really passed by the car — they all stopped and stared.

Momma and Daddy returned and were too embarrassed to claim the car. They stood with the crowd and watched as if they had never seen us before.

To this day I'm convinced that the only reason Daddy finally claimed us was because he loved his red '57 Chevy and feared for its well being. He and Momma finally slid in the front seat, and we bucked and jumped all the way to Grand-dad's. Daddy stopped the car and said, "Stand aside." He yanked open the trunk and the dog and goat made an emergency exit. That coon hound may have been stupid once, but I'll tell you one thing, he didn't make the same mistake twice. That was the last time Daddy was able to get him into the trunk!

"I Think He's Sick"

I'm sure some of you have noticed this, but men don't like to go to the doctor, even when they're half dead. I've been around men all my life—first my daddy and my brothers, and now my husband.

My daddy would pull his own teeth rather than go to a dentist. As the result, every other tooth in his head is removable. He broke his arm once and was forced to go to a doctor. They put a lovely cast on his arm, and eight days later Daddy took his hand saw and cut it off, never to have a cast again. This is the same man who now has a son who is a doctor and a daughter who is a nurse. I've never bothered asking the one who's the doctor, but I'd be willing to bet his stethoscope that he hates to go to a doctor.

My husband had a cold that settled in his chest. He was keeping me up all night by his coughing. One morning, on the verge of collapse from lack of sleep, I said, "You need to see a doctor." He said, "Well, you go find me one and I'll look at him." I decided that a chest cold was well deserved. When I tried to make a doctor's appointment, he said, "They're all too young." I said, "They may be young when you get sick, but by the time I get you to go, they'll be middle-aged."

Our son begs to go to a doctor if he gets a hangnail. But you can rest assured that somewhere between high school and thirty he will decide only to see a doctor if carried on a stretcher.

"I'm on My Way"

When this man of mine calls me at the end of the day and says, "I'm on my way," I march straight to the stove, turn it off, and pick up a magazine. There have been days I could have knitted a sweater after he said, "I'm on my way." I don't want you to get the wrong impression; he's a very thoughtful person. Always calling to let me know his plans, such as "I'm on my way." Those are the days I send a search party looking for him. Those are the days that those photo sessions that were supposed to last forty-five minutes to an hour, last five hours.

There are evenings when he arrives home, and I put the casserole in the center of the table. Rather than sit down to eat, we walk slowly around the table.

"What is it?"

"Turkey Almond, your favorite."

"It would have been delicious, I'm sure."

"Yes, it was one of my finer efforts," I say mournfully. "The little black things sticking up . . . those were the almonds."

We pay our last respects before scraping the remains down the garbage disposal and breaking open the bologna.

"I Know Exactly Where We Are"

There you are in the car—113 miles out of the way—and *he* won't ask for directions. He just passed the Last Chance gas station. The last chance to ask a living human person, "Where in the samhill are we?"

He's as lost as last year's Easter egg, but the last thing he'll do is admit it.

You sit there gripping a road map, and the sweat from your palms erases half the road on whatever state you happen to be lost in. You don't dare open your mouth. You did that an hour ago, and he drove another sixty-two miles in the wrong direction to prove to you he knows *exactly* where he is.

Relax and enjoy the drive. You get to see more of America than you bargained for when you're married to a man like this. This is most likely the same man who takes you and your 2.7 children on an 850-mile vacation without stopping to go to the restroom.

The children will pleadingly inquire, "When are we going to stop, Daddy?" He'll say, "Just over the next hill." And you drive over the next hill . . . and the next . . . and the next . . .

He may never notice, but upon arrival at your long-awaited destination, he has to use a crow bar to pry you from the front seat, because your skin is embedded in the vinyl seat covers. He also may not notice that you don't stand up straight for two days.

It is children of these types of fathers who develop a new phobia: Fathercarphobia — the fear of getting into the car with their father.

The famous lines from our marriages become the things that make us laugh or groan at just their mention. Years from now when all our children are grown, they will spin yarns with their friends about *their* family's quirks. In turn those young adults marry and create their own famous lines or revive the ones they grew up with. So, in a sense, our famous lines are part of our heritage. We pass them on.

NIP 'N' TUCK — KEEPING IT TOGETHER FOREVER

Fitness and Aging

*P*lease! Don't tell me about one more miracle diet! Don't show me any more pictures of models so skinny they'd get stretch marks from a pimple. I believe in keeping it together as long as I can find "it." I also believe that a woman shouldn't be too skinny. Flesh is sensual, and this body of mine intends to keep a little flesh on it as long as possible.

I also refuse to look at one more "makeover" of an already gorgeous person. Don't tell me all those mysterious celebrity fitness secrets. If I had a personal fitness expert who came into the privacy of my home every day and held a gun on me, I could do my own fitness video, too!

No one has to tell us when it's time to lose a few pounds. It just takes a few little hints, like when your tummy is so large you can no longer reach the sink to wash dishes and you're not pregnant.

I'll know it's time to diet when my thighs are so large I get stuck going through a doorway or if I step on an escalator that refuses to go!

I've tried everything to lose my thighs. Exercise has been a part of my life since high school. I jogged in place until a hole fell through our bedroom floor. I did leg lifts until I had bruises larger than my thighs. I practiced visualization, imagining my thighs on Nancy Reagan. The pounds never left my body, but she began to look heavier.

Actress Jaclyn Smith said in an interview that she prevents flabby thighs by tightening her muscles in between scenes. I tried that too. Have you ever tried walking with your thighs and buttocks all squenched up? Not too bad if you don't mind walking like Frankenstein.

Everybody has a different remedy. I think we should have our thighs tightly wrapped at age six just like the Japanese used to wrap feet.

When it comes to thighs, some of the differences between men and women are unfair. Have you ever heard a group of men bemoaning their expanding thighs? My husband doesn't even know where his are, because there are none on his entire body. His legs run straight from the hip to the knee — no thighs! I'm personally offended by this gender difference.

A man's legs never turn to flab. It doesn't matter if he is eighty-nine pounds overweight — he'll have firm legs. A woman's legs turn to peanut butter, the crunchy kind. I've been working out since the seventh grade and I'm only one step ahead of peanut butter.

If you ask your husband to help you curb your eating, you'd better be sure you mean it. During one such time, I said to him, "I want you to stand by me and do whatever you have to do to keep me from eating." The next night, I was in the kitchen face down in a bag of chocolate chip cookies. After he wiped the accusing expression off his face, he said, "Give me those cookies. What do you think you're doing?"

"You get your hands off these," I growled.

"I don't believe this. Just last night, you made me promise to do anything short of deadly force to keep you from eating."

"I was just testing to see if you were paying attention."

Okay, I do occasionally lapse into irresponsible behavior, but I'm in good company.

"Face Lift in a Jar"

Somebody out there thinks we're all crazy. The copy of one advertisement reads, "Face lift in a jar—only $39.95 to a new face in just days." Anothers says, "Firm thighs in thirty days or your money back!" Women spend a lot of time and *more* than a lot of money trying to keep it together. "It" in this case usually means our faces, although now we spend another fortune on health spas to keep the rest of "it" together.

So far, I've never met anyone who will confess to having tried these wondrous cures for aging. Aging is apparently one of those facts of life we almost refuse to accept. There's a lot of pressure on us these days. Every year we watch while dozens of celebrities grow younger. Their eyebrows get higher, their eyes get rounder, and their wrinkles disappear like magic. Their faces seem frozen in space.

Somewhere, just short of all of those miracle cures, are things we can do to protect and care for these delightful, though fragile, bodies. But we can't remain young forever. When people ask how old I am, I say, "I'm somewhere between being smacked on the bottom and walking with a cane, and I love every minute of it."

Bedtime Beauty

Last year, I attended a women's retreat with ladies from my church. Bedtime was a real eye-opener. If I had ever entertained the thought that all women dressed pretty much the same at bedtime, the evening shattered that notion. The bed-time costumes were so clever that I took notes.

There was a lady bringing back a tradition from too many years past — the chenille robe. A purple chenille robe. You remember those robes with large bumps all over them, made like bedspreads you see hanging along the roadside of tourist traps. The kind of places where you can see a live bear, wrestle an alligator, buy yourself a set of dishes, a corn cob pipe or — a bathrobe. A robe like this would be guaranteed to put an amorous husband into a semitrance-like state. I called this one the "catatonic purple snoozer."

The outfit that surprised me most was the pink sleeper — a suit three and a half inches thick with feet in it. This is a must for any woman who has all the right parts, but is determined not to show them. There's not a man alive who would try to find his way through that sort of protection. I called this one the "burglar-proof chastity suit."

The inventiveness of the group was endless. The next one was straight from Frederick's of Possum Holler: a tee shirt with men's boxer shorts, black leotards, and heavy wool socks.

Several women were wearing varying versions of the same outfit. The "Austin City Limits" tee shirt with gold sweat pants was real popular. This was obviously a Country & Western peignoir set purchased at Willie Nelson's Lingerie & Tractor Supply Store.

Now we come to my favorite ensemble from the weekend. This lady had to be special, and I felt myself being drawn to her. She wore a satin gown. It had been lovely in its day. I said *had* been. It was in tatters. Let me be more specific: It was in shreds. I am talking about holes you could read the Sunday paper through. And she was wearing long underwear beneath it. I could not control myself. The gown was too much for me, and as Minnie Pearl would say, my curiosity got the best of me.

Trying to be subtle, I said, "Have you noticed that your gown has holes in it?" She just smiled a long, slow, private smile. After several moments, she said wistfully, even romantically, "Yes. This is what I was wearing on our twenty-fifth wedding anniversary—the night the furnace blew up. And I've been wearing it ever since."

It may be that some women choose clothes like they would choose armor plate. Kind of like the woman who said, "When I don't want my man to mess with me, I put Noxema on my face, and Vick's salve up my nose."

Bedtime Isn't Necessarily Beauty Time

This subject of what we do to our bodies at bedtime began to fascinate me. There must be some explanation for all of the extremes we go through to cover our bodies.

What is it that causes us to be so dissatisfied with ourselves that we spend no small fortune trying to defy our bodies? Does it have anything to do with, getting older? Do we like ourselves less that when we first married? Do we have more "bends" than "curves"? Are we afraid our husbands won't love us if they see us? Maybe it's all the weird things that happen to a lady's body as she gets older, like veins and wrinkles and cellulite. (Cellulite is what you see when you look down and your whole body looks like thermal underwear.)

My best friends and I joke about checking in together for face lifts. We would go into a clinic together, then come out and see if our husbands could pick us out of a crowd. We tease about it. That's probably as far as it will ever go. I even have a friend who is prematurely gray completely. She is gorgeous and has never tried to cover it up with brown hair from a bottle. This and other aspects of life take deep-down confident acceptance.

Deep-Down Confident Aging

There are some things that make us wonder why God does them the way He does — like old age. I'll be honest. I would rather be thirty-nine years old for forty years and die of exhaustion in my sleep, preferably with all my teeth securely in my mouth, than age normally. Somehow, I just know God didn't intend us to have teeth sleep in a glass at night and smile at us first thing in the morning from the bedside table.

My friends and I are changing together. I see the character of living touching our faces, and I like it. They look great to me. Better than they used to! Their faces reflect the character of babies born and sleep lost while caring for them, and laughter, lots of laughter. On their faces I see the traces of sorrow that leave a special tenderness, of crises and victories, sunshine and memories. My best friends are like that, and I love them for it. They are happy with who they are, and I'd be willing to bet their husbands are happy with them too.

Someday, years from now, my husband and I will be sitting on the porch and I'll say, "Darlin', things just aren't like they used to be." And he'll reply, "No, things aren't even *where* they used to be." And I'll say, "The only thing I have left that's soft and round is my gums when my teeth are out."

He tells me that I haven't changed since we married. Sometimes, he says I even look better than when we married. I think with charm like that he should run for political office and that his bifocals need cleaning. (I also think he's the kindest person I've ever had the pleasure of knowing!)

He believes that a person's wrinkles, the lines on their face, are the very character of their appearance. He believes they have earned those wrinkles through living. This may be true, but too often we don't want to acknowledge that.

I've been associated with show business for several years and have seen vanity from a less than desirable perspective.

A classic example is the woman who went to a photographer. He photographed her, but she wasn't pleased. She wanted magic. She didn't want to look like what she saw in the mirror. She went to another studio where they used diffusion and finally airbrushed away every last trace of her true appearance. She no longer resembled herself and she was happy.

The truth is, we need more than our pictures retouched. We need to have our lives retouched. Only a heavenly Father can do that, and that's exactly the sort of business He is in. His retouching never damages the product, only improves and polishes it. His retouching does not cover up; it opens up and exposes the best in every person. It doesn't cost money and the results are guaranteed to last forever.

True love goes past the skin of life to the heart of our beings where the human personality lives. It can keep on loving through wrinkles, bends, and alterations in appearance, past the age when a woman's thighs turn to peanut butter, and a man's hair turns gray and turns loose at the same time.

God, the heavenly Father, creates and plans all of life — even "surprises" are not accidental. So, I've come to the conclusion that aging is no accident either.

THE NINTH WONDER
OF THE WORLD
Intimacy

$\mathcal{M}$y husband is full of helpful suggestions for this book. He saw me working on this particular topic and said, "Maybe more couples would be blessed with intimacy if they went backpacking on their honeymoons." (This will go on record as one of the least intelligent remarks he has made.) Then he sat down to wait for my reply looking real satisfied with himself.

Without pausing to look at him, I said, "If more couples began their life together in a two-man tent, there wouldn't be five out of a thousand who would survive to celebrate their first anniversary."

So, what is intimacy? Intimacy is not created by living in a one-room apartment, or a two-man tent. There must be more to it than being in the same room, because a couple can live in a one-room apartment and be emotionally disconnected,

Intimacy is more than having your underwear in the same drawer as his shorts. It's more than getting your "parts" together. Does it just happen like a car wreck you can't remember or taking your first step or saying that first word? Is it something you decide like, "Oh, let's be intimate today?"

Someone told me of a woman who wouldn't undress in front of her husband after fifteen years of marriage. Yet, they had children—beats the cornbread out of me. You can't get children without what would seem to be a very intimate kind of experience. The kind of intimate experience married people have—sex. So, intimacy must be something other than sex.

Some couples seem to share secrets that the rest of us aren't in on. They laugh at the mention of a word, a place, or a favorite expression. They look at each other—often. They're unafraid of what they will see in the other person's eyes or what will be seen in their own. They seem like separate halves of the same picture, making up a whole, exposed to each other like film with a definite image. Intimacy can be different things to different people, but every human being desires to be known, loved, and accepted at the innermost level.

My husband made a profound statement about marriage the other day: "Marriage is one body living in two separate skins." Looking at it that way could probably help create intimacy in a marriage.

For all sorts of reasons, many couples don't have this kind of oneness: differences in background, the kind of rearing we had, the level or lack of intimacy in our childhood homes. Many men break out in a rash if you just mention the word *intimacy.* Just say the word or begin a tender conversation, and you'll see the back of your husband getting smaller, walking away.

But men aren't the only ones who avoid intimacy. Many women also walk away from closeness. Behind this evasion of intimacy lies fear of being hurt, or fear of problems we can't define, much less understand. This would be a sad subject if there were no hope, but there is. I know of couples who, through proper counseling, began to peel away the layers of camouflage they had spent a lifetime acquiring.

They began to lose their fear of sharing their innermost thoughts. They learned to listen to each other without judging the content of what is said or the person saying it. They learned ultimately, through lots of trying and failing and trying again, to replace old patterns with new, healthier ones.

Someone whose marriage has gone through a tremendous metamorphosis in recent years said, "I don't know which of us has changed the most because we're *both* so different now." This change began with one person's willingness to adapt, which eventually opened the door for both of them to grow and blend together.

One lady said to me that if she and her husband didn't have the children to talk about, they wouldn't have anything to say to each other. These two people *must* have talked before they married, or did they just look at each other thinking words would come later? No, they talked, but somewhere along the way, flossing their teeth together may have become their most intimate moment.

Sharing's Not Dividing — It's Multiplying Life

You can't share your life without talking to each other. I know people who have tried it, but it just doesn't work. Anything less is just existing, and for most of us, existing isn't enough.

Occasionally I'm reminded that many couples spend very little time actually talking. One evening at a church dinner, my husband and I were waiting to go into the dining room and were in a corner talking. A friend came over to us and said, "You two must not have seen each other for a while."

We looked up, a bit surprised, and I said, "No, actually, we have worked together all day today." Then the friend was the one surprised. "And you *still* have something to say to each other?" she asked.

What happened to the reality that marriage is a sharing of our lives with another person? Have we entirely forgotten what it means to share? According to Webster, it means: "A portion belonging to an individual; to divide and parcel out in shares; to participate in, experience or use in common." Sharing is at its ultimate best when both partners give a lot to each other. I give a lot, I give up a lot, because I "get" so much in return. I've also given up keeping a list of whatever it was I "gave up" in order to have this thing called intimacy.

Intimacy may be nothing more than being available for an activity in which your spouse is interested. (If the favorite activity of your spouse is underwater glass blowing, and you're deathly afraid of water, you may be in big trouble here.) I'll readily trade all the red roses in the world for the warm, affectionate appreciation in my husband's face when I've willingly been involved in something he wanted to do— such as driving around all day while he photographs such architectural wonders as a two-hundred-year-old flour mill that collapsed ninety years ago. Depending on the weather, I can sit under a tree or in the car. I can think, dream, read, or write. I soak in the sight of my spouse doing something he truly loves to do. I admire him. He enjoys knowing that I am watching him, but you can bet your CDs he'll never say so. Some of our most romantic evenings follow days like this.

Couples who don't communicate, who don't take time for listening, sharing, and laughing, rarely have intimacy in their marriages. I have a pretty good idea that those are the marriages that end up several years down the road with one spouse walking through the door and saying, "I'm leaving. I haven't been happy for a long time." The other spouse, shocked and disillusioned over the "sudden" collapse of the marriage, claims not to have suspected a thing.

Keeping in touch, keeping sensitivity to each other alive, is what intimate moments are all about. For those moments to happen, couples need to look each other in the eye — eyeball-to-eyeball — and *listen* to what is being said. When my husband puts down his favorite photographic magazine and focuses his attention on me, I feel as if the director has said, "All quiet on the set," and "Action." That's the moment when not only do I have his eyes, but his heart as well, and the stage is set for an intimate moment.

If you create enough of those special moments, it can open the door to a more satisfying sex life.

It Pays to Advertise at Home

You would think some people have forgotten marriage is about a very close, personal, intimate relationship, that even includes sex.

My husband says it pays to advertise. He walked into our bedroom the other night and said, "How do you like my outfit?"

I said, "I love it! Definitely my favorite!" This favorite outfit is his skin. It's hard to beat. It suits him to a T. It's just his size and never goes out of style. Just seeing him in it can lead to other things. So he shows it to me every chance he gets.

Some couples allow this element of fun and adventure to be killed off early in their marriages. They become too serious about everything. Soon, one or the other of them will say, "We don't have fun any more — you've changed — what happened to you?"

Life hurls its serious side at us so quickly we have difficulty recovering from the shock. The responsibility of earning a living is serious. Rearing children is nearly fatal. It's no wonder that couples lose the element of serendipity — unexpected joy in their relationship.

Couples who still have unexpected joy in their marriage have never stopped working at it. They never stop making time for the little things and when necessary for planning their "spontaneous" moments.

The Thick and Thin

Many long-time married couples have my deepest admiration. When the subject of marriage comes up, there is a flicker of fire in their eyes and a laughter that says they have lived through the thick and thin of life and survived to tell about it. They have paid their dues, and they are glad of it.

They glance at each other with a knowing look that recalls the times they could have thrown in the towel along with the marriage license. There is a familiarity that comes across as the deepest kind of intimacy.

This familiarity comes from sharing those narrow escapes in marriage — from communicating your way through the misunderstandings that are a natural part of the process. True intimacy comes from learning to accept the fact that the person you have pledged before the Good Lord to spend the rest of your life with grinds his teeth all night or snores so loudly the neighbors call in the middle of the night.

Is Intimacy Possible After the Children Come Along?

One of the rewards of achieving a deeper level of intimacy will be a more satisfying sex life. This means you will be spending more time behind the closed door of your own bedroom. Like everything else having to do with a family, one thing leads to another.

The next thing you will have to deal with is your children saying, "Mommy, what were all of those strange noises you and Daddy were making last night?"

This particular question caused me to explain a previously nonexisting asthma condition and to lie about rescuing the cat from the bed springs. Children's bodies may go to sleep, but their ears walk around in the night. If you're like us and living in a very old house with old-fashioned large keyholes in the doors, you might consider moving.

If your children range in age from newborn to two years of age, I suggest you move to Africa. Families of apes are available in most parts of the continent to take care of children in this age bracket while you do your thing. If your children are older than two, the apes may want no part of them, which means you'll have to resort to other measures.

If your home has a medieval decor, you might like a moat filled with piranhas surrounding your bedroom to discourage intrusions. I said *your* bedroom because it is most important that you and your spouse keep control of the drawbridge.

Having your doorknob connected to an electric fence generator is an effective deterrent against unexpected entry, as is a trap door concealed under a rug.

If the children have "listened in," there are embarrassing questions in the beginning and knowing looks combined with an occasional snicker at the older stages. The sooner you deal with listening, the better.

The most elementary technique for counteracting this problem is "aural camouflage," better known as noise. Music is a good way to start. However, avoid the Rolling Stones — the listeners will know you are up to no good.

If you are in desperate need of a romantic getaway, you might try leasing a motor home with a deaf chauffeur.

All of this is to say that even if we're blessed with a deep level of intimacy when we marry, it's necessary that we work to preserve it. If we don't work at it, especially after the children come along, intimacy can do a disappearing act that makes the magician David Copperfield look like an amateur.

EIGHT

"THE BEST THINGS IN LIFE ARE FREE"
And Other Myths

*T*he basic premise of this statement *may be* true—may be. Or it might have been true when whatever demented genius said it; but today, if anything in life is free, you can bet it costs a lot just to keep it going.

It's like the young man who went to the courthouse to purchase a marriage license. "How much does a marriage license cost?" he asked. The man behind the counter, looking over the top of his bifocals, said, "Fifteen dollars and your income for life."

The air we breathe is not free anymore. We pay good money to maintain our cars so we don't exceed pollution levels. It doesn't cost anything to stand back and look at the Eiffel Tower, but round trip airfare for two on the Concorde from America is about $10,000.

At first, you might think watching television is free. But no. We sit there and watch 3,460 commercials a week and then rush right out and purchase all those products that television convinces us we can't live without. So if those things aren't free, what does that leave us? A smile? On certain streets in certain cities, if you smile at the wrong person, you can get your face rearranged for free — but the medical bills will cost.

A Sunday afternoon ride would be free if you could take it without your car. Even bicycling has changed. We bought our son a $200 bicycle. He went out and ran into a parked car, costing us $400 in repairs to the car.

The year of our greatest financial crisis was a long one. Weeks stretched into months when there just wasn't enough work and, consequently, never enough money. When you're in a marriage where both partners are not only self-employed but are also creative people, you learn the real meaning of having your backs to the wall. Our backs weren't to the wall, they were nailed to the studs!

During this particular time we were enjoying a spring afternoon sitting in our antique rockers on the front porch practicing for life in the poor house. I said, "It's amazing to be so happy when everything seems to be falling down around us."

He said, "Yeah, they sang on the deck of the Titanic, too!"

"Love Will Get You Through
the Times with No Money"

I've done extensive research on this phrase, and all I can say is that I've never been able to walk through the checkout lane at the supermarket and pass my wedding ring over the scanner. The ring is a symbol of eternal love, and it should be worth something when you need a new dress or a carton of milk.

I tried to hock my wedding ring during a dry spell of the green stuff. I took it to the finest jeweler in town. She looked at my symbol of eternal love with one of those magnifying things for about two seconds, smacked my symbol back in my hand, and said rather haughtily, "It has a speck of carbon in it." This woman obviously was not a romantic.

If love could get you through the lean times, no couple carrying a baby would ever have to pay for anything. Babies smile at everybody. They even smile at people who haven't smiled since their first-grade school picture.

The Beatles wrote an eighty-five-measure, four-minute-long song with only one lyric, "All you need is love . . . love is all you need." RIGHT! An easy idea to believe in when you're worth $40 trillion at the bank.

If this were true, all newlyweds would have to do to purchase their first home is walk up to the mortgage banking officer and the glow of their love would close the loan instantly. You can rest assured that when a couple leaves for the honeymoon, stuffed to the gills with love, it won't pay the hotel bill for their trip to Hawaii, Florida, or even the cheap hotel down the street.

There is, hopefully, never more love than when a baby is born. This kind of love should make a difference in the cruel financial world. When the loving couple's firstborn enters the picture, the scene at hospital admissions should go like this:

"We're here to have a baby!"

"Fine. Just fill out these forms," says the clerk. "Include all the lines marked with an X and give us all information as to who the responsible and loving parties are. Just sign below if you will love this child for the rest of its life. That's all we need."

My entire life has been costly. If I had been fortunate enough to give birth to my own children, I can tell you the exact scenario. After plopping the little bundle on my tummy, the delivery nurse would have said, "She has an irregular gum line. Take some advice and begin saving for braces."

"Cheaper by the Dozen"

One of my lifelong curiosities has been to meet the person who coined this phrase. That person never walked into McDonald's and said, "Give me twelve Big Macs, twelve large orders of fries, and twelve large Cokes," to say nothing of taking twelve people to an expensive restaurant.

It's beyond my wildest imagination that it may have ever been cheaper. I do realize there was a day when children didn't go to the nearest mall, pick out their own clothes, and pay for them with their parent's Visa card. In bygone days, the wife and mother beat a path from the kitchen stove to the sewing machine where she stitched every thread on each and every piece of clothing the family wore. My guess is that if the author of "Cheaper By The Dozen" had bothered asking his own mom and dad before coining that phrase, it would have never been minted.

"Two Can Live As Cheaply As One"

This would be a great way for an overweight couple to lose their extra pounds. They could order only one dinner when eating out or fix only enough for one serving when dining at home.

My husband and I probably could split our meals with no problem at all. Neither of us would miss that extra food. However, I am married to a guy who has spent his lifetime looking for Dairy Queens and knows exactly where each and every one is located all over America. This is not the type of guy who would roll into a Dairy Queen, order half of a chocolate shake, and walk away happy.

He is the generous type; he lets me wear his sweaters and shares a hair dryer with me. We've even been known to take a shower . . . together. But—make no mistake—the day will never come when he'll give me half of his chocolate shake. There are just some things in life that you *must* have two of, and there's no arguing the point. A toothbrush was never meant to be shared. That's for the couple who truly wants to share everything, including gum disease.

Things that used to be free now cost a quarter. We went to Wal-Mart. They have a new toy. You put a quarter in a machine and discover your correct weight for your height. We put a quarter in, and I now know what I'm overweight, my biorhythms are low, my brain is nearly gone, and I have a low intelligence quotient. Now, I'm also depressed. So we went home to watch television. My husband said that I was sitting too close to him on the sofa, and he was hot. Probably afraid my intelligence quotient would rub off on him. I said, "My biorhythms are down and you're being mean to me."

"I am not," he said.

"You are too mean!" I repeated, "—and you're ugly, too!" By this time, he was laughing at me. (His biorhythms were high and his intelligence topped out.)

Some days are just like that. But I'll tell you the truth—I wish I had my quarter back.

Balance My What?

Before we married, I had seen a checkbook—once. I thought it was a thin appointment book. Then I learned that all you had to do was sign at the bottom and those pages worked like "real money." I thought I'd discovered Fort Knox. SERIOUSLY.

Then I began to get "personal" mail from the bank every day. All the numbers had a minus sign in front of them. That seemed to me an appropriate way to subtract the checks I'd written, so I just collected them thinking I would add them up later.

"Later" came when my husband arrived home from work unusually early one day. He was not smiling. He said some things that hurt my feelings. When I asked him to write to Congress to extend our debt ceiling, his eyes began to bulge right out of his head.

He asked me if I'd ever heard of balancing a checkbook. I said I had plenty of checks, but I didn't know where to find the balance. He said, "No kidding, Sherlock." That led to a discussion of mathematics, and I began to perspire. I told him I had math hysteria and didn't want to talk about it any more. He took a long walk *and* my checkbook!

Later on, I had a credit card. He didn't have a chance to take it away from me. I used it so much it overheated and set my purse on fire. That took care of that!

Now my money is rationed, mainly because there's never enough of it. I've come a long way since those early days. Men and women all over America should be grateful to me. I inspired a new banking service called "overdraft protection."

But the best protection is a good plan. Today it is a well-published fact that finances top the list of things couples argue about most frequently. Fortunately, there are good financial counselors ready and waiting to help put together a plan. People who take the time to plan usually have less to argue about than those without one. When there simply isn't enough money with or without a plan, we should tackle our finances with the determination to be responsible and a willingness to do without until we can do better. We tackle the problem, not each other.

In this previous story it may appear that I was the problem when in reality the problem was simply my ignorance.

Well, I guess the secret is out: falling in love is costly. So, it's a good idea to get it right the first time. When you do, the price will never be too great.

ABOUT AS
GLAMOROUS
AS A BUNION

PMS

*P*MS. PMS is a condition that is now taken seriously by many physicians who have taken time to educate themselves. For many years, I searched for a doctor who might have some sort of knowledge about this mysterious pattern my body and emotions took each month.

Pre-menstrual syndrome is when once a month your body tries to reject itself. So every month I think this should be happening to Princess Di — not a perfectly ordinary person like me.

My husband says, "There's nothing ordinary about a person who can laugh and cry simultaneously. There's not a hint of the ordinary about someone who puts empty pots on the stove and cooks them for an hour and a half whether they need it or not. Nothing ordinary about someone who spends $8.95 on a product that turns her hair bright green; then spends $150 to pay someone to fix it the way it should have been in the first place."

"Those things are not my fault. I have PMS, you know!"

"Just because you have PMS doesn't mean you have to act like you have PMS," he said.

It's a credit to my intelligence that I married a man that smart!

"Just think how boring your life could have been if you hadn't married someone with PMS," I said.

"I suppose you're right. I could have become hopelessly addicted to live studio wrestling," he said.

"Does that mean you didn't enjoy eating spaghetti off the kitchen ceiling or finding a pair of your socks in the crock pot?"

"Variety is the spice of life," he said, "but there have been a few times when the spice has pretty much been more than I could stand."

"I'm not as bad as the lady who scheduled a face lift during her pre-menstrual time, and then canceled it when the date came because she had started her period!" This kind of repartee was *close* to hurting my feelings.

He agreed with me. "No," he said, "You'd go ahead and have the face lift. Then the next time you were pre-menstrual, you'd sue the doctor for tampering with the looks God gave you." (That did it! They were hurt! I wished wrinkles would appear on his face and a mood swing would hit him that would send *him* to a gynecologist.)

Holding my shoulders as straight as I could, I said, "It's been no picnic for me either! My life is about as glamorous as a bunion and not nearly as much fun."

Following which, he said, "If the shoe had never been invented, we wouldn't have discovered the bunion." Then he walked out of the room.

A man like this could *cause* PMS.

I always try to take care of my husband, especially when I'm pre-menstrual. I do special things for him. I spent an hour trying to get the World Series on the microwave oven.

The thanks I get is a song my husband composed called "Home, Home of the Strange."

> Home, home of the strange,
> Where the husband and children, they cringe.
> Where seldom is heard an intelligent word,
> And dinner burns up on the range.

It isn't easy to have PMS in a family like mine.

Do You Have It?

You know you have PMS . . . When you look in the mirror and don't recognize yourself.

- When you pick up someone else's kids at car pool and don't notice until breakfast the next morning.

- When you go shopping and buy shoes that are two sizes too small and wear them anyway.

- When you twist your hot electric curling brush in your hair and have to cut it out.

- When the nice handsome man you married looks like the villain out of an Hitchcock film.

- When your words come out backward but make perfect sense to you.

- When your best friend finishes all of your sentences for you and you let her.

- When you cry because your husband runs over a dandelion with the lawnmower.

- When you cook a pot of fresh asparagus and eat the whole thing before dinner.

- When you serve chicken breasts stuffed with M&Ms for dinner and you're the only one who eats them.

- When even your three-year-old pats your hand and says, "It otay, Mommy. You be awrite in foo days." (Which is just what he heard his father say when they hid in the closet to have a family meeting about you behind your back.)

- When the family dog disappears for the same ten days every month.

- When UPS asks you if there's a responsible person at home.

- When your mother-in-law's Christmas present to you is a year of weekly sessions with a psychiatrist.

I don't mind having PMS any more. I just view it as a good way to keep my family on their toes. It's the least I can do to them for all the times they don't eat spinach and put mustard on their scrambled eggs, as well as other weird traits they considered to be "perfectly normal." You and I know better. The day you show me a perfectly normal person, I'll show you a doctor with a warm examining room.

PMS and DFW

PMS makes you a very resourceful person. I have stumbled upon unique ways of drawing attention to myself. My best PMS behavior occurred in the Dallas-Fort Worth airport. As an entertainer, I'd been traveling for a couple of years, and my husband had always been able to travel with me. He'd been responsible for such frightening things as maneuvering me through airports. But when I acquired my first booking agency and began to tour with greater frequency, it was no longer possible for him to accompany me.

My first major trip alone brought my usual rotten luck. I was pre-menstrual. I was to fly with my husband to DFW, and from there I was forced to continue alone. My husband was flying out of Dallas to work at another location.

He safely deposited me at the proper gate where I was supposed to wait for my flight. We hugged each other, and he started to walk away to the shuttle that would take him to another gate. In my heart, I said goodbye forever, knowing it would be the last time we ever saw each other. And right there, in front of God, fourteen thousand fellow travelers, and one stunned and embarrassed husband, I hyperventilated. I hyperventilated and cried simultaneously. Tell me that's not creative. My tears were airborne and traveling across the waiting room of one of the largest airports in America. I lived through it, learned to find my way through airports alone, and did live to see my husband again. It's a story my husband loves to tell and I let him, but I own the copyright.

Grown Men Don't Understand Crying

Most of us learned to cry when we were only two hours old or sooner. We didn't cry more than two or three times before we noticed the effect it had on our mommies. Before we reached the age of two, we had learned the effect it had on our daddies. We discovered it was a simple way to turn a grown man into a puddle.

It was so effective, in fact, that most of us decided to continue using it after marriage. After all, a husband is just another grown man. Well, he may be a grown man, but, trust me, he doesn't have the capacity to understand crying. He'll say, "Why are you crying?"

"Because."

"Because why?" he'll ask.

P-A-U-S-E. Deep breath. *"Just because!"*

"Oh," he'll say, "that explains everything. Just because."

Then my husband shakes his head and walks into another room. I accuse him of deserting me at the moment of my deepest need and slam a door. He's shaking his head and wishing he'd majored in marriage and family counseling, because he's quite sure his wife needs help.

The last thing you should do is admit to your husband that crying feels good. I know because I did. He headed for the phone book, the section listing "Physicians"; then he said, "Is this PMS talking, or do you need to see another kind of doctor?"

See, this is where having PMS can be a valuable asset. You can blame crying on it. You can say that when you cry, your PMS feels better, and he will accept *that*. But if you simply cry and have no good reason, he can't deal with it.

Or, you can fabricate a highly technical, medical-sounding reason for crying. You can borrow mine. He'll never again ask why you're doing it. I just say, "This is recommended for purging the biofibrilators of the metzomusculartors and semi-rignifilters."

This sort of answer will be accepted without question. But a simple "it makes me feel better," and you're a candidate for therapy.

If you're looking for the answer to these and other such mysterious maladies, you won't find it in this book. You might try calling an 800 number, but if a man answers—hang up.

Sanity Comes and Goes

So that's how PMS feels. There were times I questioned my sanity only to have sanity return the next day, and I would once again feel like the picture of stability and energy.

But my highs were high, my lows were low, and there weren't many days in between.

It's not pleasant to wake up feeling that your children are impostors, your husband is purposely trying to hurt your feelings, and that your best friends have turned on you — all while knowing in your inner being that none of it's real.

Nonetheless, it *feels* real when your body feels like it weighs 380 pounds, and it's just too much trouble to walk from the bedroom to any room other than the one with the refrigerator.

Unfortunately for many women, doctors prescribe medications that do *nothing* to relieve PMS. Prescription medications merely create additional problems such as addiction. Then you're addicted to something you didn't need in the first place — and still have PMS.

I went to a long list of physicians — all of whom prescribed "a little something, just to help you through those difficult times." (Tranquilizers.) Does that seem like a viable solution for someone who is already walking around half dead?

I came from a home where aspirin was the only medication in the medicine cabinet. We were taught to look for solutions, not cover-ups. We were taught the importance of caring for our bodies and of not doing anything unnatural or risky to them. So when a doctor handed me a prescription for some mysterious potion, I didn't thank him. Instead I walked outside his office and tore up that little piece of paper and said, "Next!" I continued going down a list of physicians until I found one who listened to me and was interested in constructive solutions — one who didn't suggest sending me to visit a hospital for women who do strange things.

Luckily I found that there are some positive, helpful practices to ease you through difficult days. They're actually very simple: it's the old diet and exercise routine. The difficult part is making the mental decision to be doggedly determined and disciplined.

Caring for a body that is troubled by pre-menstrual syndrome means making a conscious effort to eat plenty of fresh fruits and vegetables. It means not giving in to eating bags of cookies or anything else with sugar. And caffeine aggravates PMS and should be avoided. (It can cause heart palpitations that have nothing to do with falling in love.)

Exercise has long been known to relieve stress and produce a sense of well being. Contrary to what some women think, cleaning house and chasing a two-year-old do *not* qualify as exercise. They do produce exhaustion, but have never been touted as producing euphoria, relief from stress, or cardiovascular fitness.

It isn't necessary to exercise until your muscles turn to concrete. Most fitness experts today recommend fast walking. It's easy on your joints, and you can walk with a friend while carrying on an enjoyable conversation at the same time.

I've even seen young mothers pushing baby strollers at a fast speed on the outdoor track where I walk. I highly recommend it, but you may want to invest in a crash helmet for the little one! Fast walking seems to give me an "all over" workout and when exercising regularly, I seem to sleep better at night (rather than in church or at a meeting!).

My pastor is especially appreciative of this since I sit on the first row in the choir.

IT'S NOT A NEW FOREIGN CAR

A Career

*W*hen the hosts of morning tele-
vision, Jane Pauley and Joan Lunden, started having babies,
the ratings of both shows went up. People like me began tun-
ing in to both programs just to see how these lovely women
would handle the pressure.

Wouldn't you just love to see Jane Pauley show up on
camera with a blob of slobber on her blouse and say to her
viewers, "I have no apology to make; the baby threw up on
me on the way to the studio." It would be a public service if
just once Joan Lunden would come in looking green around
the gills, fall dead asleep on camera, wake up with a start,
and say, "Please forgive me, but the baby woke up seventeen
times last night, the nanny walked out, and my husband slept
through the whole thing." Every mommy in America would
stand up and cheer!

Many of you, upon learning that your first little tot was
on the way, made the decision to leave behind the world of
heels and hose, high finance, and performance reviews. You
turned in your notice, enjoyed your farewell party, and

promised to bring your bundle of joy by the office as soon as possible. You then walked out the front door and drove home to begin a crash course in rude awakenings and new beginnings.

You fantasized about having unhurried afternoons before the baby arrived to leisurely shop your favorite boutiques. Then the first crash hits — you no longer have the money to shop your favorite boutiques. You no longer have an income, period! In fact, you may have to beg for money just to buy the Snickers you crave every afternoon at 2:15. You determine that somehow you *will* survive, and this is the very moment you begin the habit of raiding your husband's pockets for change after he goes to sleep.

When your baby is eight weeks old, you wake up one morning feeling 103 years old, your joints are stiff, and the skin on your face has sagged. You stagger into the baby's room and hang your head over the crib. You feel for all the world like you are at death's door, and the thought passes through you mind that you should have named guardians for this little mouth. All of a sudden she looks up at you, stops crying, her eyes focus on your baggy face — and she smiles. Your heart turns to strawberry Jell-o. This baby doesn't care if you don't wear all the latest designer fashions. You can nurse her every day for six months wearing a finely tailored business suit, and she won't be impressed at all.

Babies are not discriminating either. They will decorate all your favorite silk dresses with accessories that won't cost a penny, and most of them come off only with the dry cleaner's help.

Compared to a Two-Year-Old, Even the Boss Looks Good

A very strange thing happens to a mother when her child reaches the age of two. Three months of the "terrible twos" and you suddenly remember the career you gave up. You don't remember the boss's bad breath or his penchant for a cigar after lunch. You will remember only one fact — there are *no children* at the office.

A career is not a new make of a foreign car. A career is another name for more work than any mother really needs. But at that very moment, while your tennis shoe is mired in peanut butter on the kitchen floor and your little ankle-biter is following you around perfecting the only words he knows — "MINE" and "NO!" — suddenly, going back to work sounds like an idea made in heaven.

A career in the sixties was something we talked about in the dormitory late at night. To be perfectly honest, we talked more about guys than we did careers. Here we are in the eighties and that trend seems to have totally reversed. Women spend more time talking career than planning home.

We have been conditioned to the eighties theme of "having it all." No one, anywhere, ever, really has it all. At various times we have a little more of "this" and a little less of "that." So what we're all searching for is — balance. Balance is that mysterious condition that occurs when our priorities are in order. Balance brings about a certain sense of peace and the awareness that "this may be difficult, but it's 'right.'"

There are other reasons why the daydream of "having it all" builds. You can't have a conversation with a two-year-old. Don't kid yourself — they understand completely every word *we* say to them. But *they* are smarter than we are and will only answer with words designed to cause complete chaos.

Occasionally, I meet that rare child who has managed to carry the terrible two syndrome well into kindergarten. By this time, the poor mother and father are still married, still living in the same house, but are trying to figure some way to see the child only on weekends.

I place my admiration at the feet of any mother who chooses to remain at home when her children are young. She *chooses* the toughest career and calling of all by remaining at home. She chooses to be the one to wipe all of the dirty noses, wipe away all the tears, plan the birthday parties, and watch them take those first steps.

I'm well aware that not everyone will marry and have a home. But for those who marry and bring children into the world, who gave us permission to change our priorities? Those dreams inside each of us don't have to be tucked away forever. Scores of women *and* men are discovering ways to remain closer to home while fulfilling a desired goal and earning a living. These same men and women are answering some tough questions and *temporarily* rearranging their priorities.

Does an eighties child have fewer needs than a child of the fifties? Does a child of the eighties recognize the difference between being comforted by a day care worker and being cradled in its own mother's arms?

The eighties slogan "Having It All" was written with only adults in mind. The children of those who supposedly have it all, in fact, have so little. A child does not have the capacity to postpone its needs until it is more convenient for its parents. A child does not have the capacity to store up all of his or her thoughts that need to be shared until the end of the day. The mother who has it all comes home frazzled to face children who are hungry for more than dinner.

None of this is intended to cause anguish in the hearts of those of you whose circumstances absolutely mandate that you work. You are doing *all* you can do and many of you, given the choice, would gladly remain at home with your children. Many working mothers don't really choose to work. But under the financial pressures of this day and age, they often feel guilty if they *don't* bring in a paycheck.

If you are one of the women for whom working *is* optional, maybe this is simply a new beginning. A place to take stock of your priorities. A place to begin rethinking the question, "Is it really worth it, after all?"

These particular pages are for those who may be putting comfort, personal needs, plans and desires for things above the needs of those precious little ones you've been given. This chapter is dedicated to tired mothers who stay at home by choice. It is dedicated to all the nursery rhymes sung by a mother while she rocks her young to sleep. It is dedicated to all the stories read and millions of questions answered in a day's time. It is dedicated to the commitment to rearing secure, whole, confident children who will remember childhood with happy memories in a loving home.

ELEVEN

AN ENDANGERED SPECIES

Romance

I was a late bloomer, but there were times my parents thought I was a bloomin' idiot.

An early bloomer usually blossoms early, falls off the vine, and marries early. I was definitely not one of those. I've always been a late bloomer — that's when everybody else has everything else before you have anything else.

In my early years, my braces stuck out farther than my chest. The braces came off and my teeth are now straight, but some things never change.

In the first years of high school when other girls were dating, I was reading books and playing basketball. I thought the other girls were terribly popular, and more than a few times, envied them. They were beautiful when I had acne. They seemed to know just what clothes to wear. They read magazines when I'd never heard of fashion. I wouldn't say that my parents were strict in those days, but I was the only girl at my sophomore class picnic in a skirt. I was allowed to play basketball, but I drew the line — I would not let Mother sew a ruffle on the legs of my uniform!

I didn't date a lot during high school. This was due largely to the baby sister whom I had wanted for years and who took it solely upon herself to approve the men in my life. I returned from a date one evening with someone I had not dated before. She performed her streaking routing (she was four years old), pranced up to him, put her hands on her naked hips and said, "My momma don't like you and I don't either!" Needless to say I went away to college.

During my college years, my friends and I talked about getting married. We even took marriage and family courses. But to this day, I can't find anyone who remembers the contents of the textbooks. We only thought about marriage, and when you said it, the word had a certain sound to it, spoken as if in a trance (which is the state of mind in which Daddy accused me of being when those first grades came in!).

The truth is, in those days we thought too little of marriage and too much of romance. Romance (I've heard this somewhere before.) is like a paper lantern left standing out in the pouring rain. After a while the light goes out and you're left with a soggy, plain brown bag.

Something Wishy-Washy About Romance

My husband and I fell in love in the grocery store. Somewhere between aisles C and D, we stopped contemplating cans of tuna and began contemplating each other. That's true romance.

I had no car in those days, and he was a good friend to me — always checking to see when I needed to go to the laundry or grocery store. Somewhere around the fifteenth consecutive month of trips to the wishy-washy, we fell in love.

We never had to worry whether we were merely affected by good food, candlelight, and soft music. The only food I could afford in those days was tuna, and the only music in the wishy-washy was the rhythm of a washing machine off balance. There was no candlelight. We definitely fell in love in the glare of fluorescent lights with an absence of atmosphere. But it was so romantic at the time.

I'll admit that I've since grown calloused. When he tried to take me back to the wishy-washy to celebrate falling in love, I was not impressed. He wanted to return to the scene of the crime, but I was hoping for some candlelight and soft music. Just talking about the memory of the wishy-washy and grocery store would have been romantic enough for me. I pass by the tuna every week at the grocery store and have never again had a shiver run down my spine.

Romance — What Is It?

Before we married, I mentioned that I was NOT the flower-type. Mainly because the only flowers I ever received came from someone whose affection I did not return. So, I changed the name on the card and had them delivered to my college roommate. She was thrilled until two days later when she saw the back of the card, which had my name scratched out.

From that one occasion, I decided I was not a "flowers person."

I casually mentioned this to my husband BEFORE we married. He believed me. Would you believe that he has *never* sent me flowers? Just because of something I said! The moral of this story is that before you make rash statements, consider this: your husband may have a memory.

But my husband does understand romance. On one of our anniversaries, he bought me one of those copper wire chickens that you hang up in the kitchen and put onions in.

"Lovely," I said. "I've been searching everywhere for one of these!" (Lightening didn't strike me for misrepresenting the truth.)

He had the nerve to look serious while giving me something like this: "I see you fail to see the significance of this."

"Oh, no! I believe in cooking with lots of onions, and the chicken is primary to the survival of Americans everywhere."

"Oh, come on," he said. "You know, the traditional gift for the seventh anniversary is copper."

See, that's romantic.

I had a friend whose thoughtful husband went to the trouble of locating two railroad spikes for their eleventh anniversary. You put two railroad spikes together and they form the number "11," and the traditional gift for the eleventh year is iron. Isn't that romantic!? Somehow, she failed to see the deep romantic significance, too.

Romance is an attitude of the heart. It leads us to do unexpected things at unexpected times. It is *not* romantic for a man to show up unannounced at dinner with three out-of-town business associates. That certainly qualifies as the unexpected, but not for romance.

It isn't romantic for a wife to appear in her husband's office with a picnic lunch on the day of the most crucial board meeting of the year. Somehow, I don't think he'd be able to appreciate it! That, too, capitalizes on the element of surprise, but won't win any awards for good sense.

My sister has been married a year now. They are still newlyweds. I just don't know what she would do without me to call every day to tell me how perfectly wonderful "he" is. He is so romantic—everything he does is romantic. She called me only this weekend to tell me that he had split six ricks of firewood and that she never thought she would meet ANYONE better at cutting wood than our daddy. "Oh, Sissy," she said, "he was just wonderful. You just wouldn't believe it!"

Yes, indeed. Frankly, I'm relieved. I was a little worried when their first major purchase was a Lazy Boy recliner.

So, you see romance is different things to different people. If to you romance is when your husband remembers to send flowers, then at times when there is no money for flowers, there would be no romance.

Is It the Things You Say?

Many women interpret romance as the things men say to them like: "Your eyes are like the haze around the purple moon." The way I see it, he just told her that her mascara is smudged. That's not romance.

There have been times when it was romantic to eat a hot dog with all the fixin's. Just knowing we had the money to buy a hot dog was pretty exciting, too.

Romance can be many things in marriage. Too many people see romance as having only to do with all the exciting and *spectacular* things we do for each other. You know, flowers, candlelight dinners for two, moonlight walks in the park, surprise trips to the Bahamas.

Couples who have truly romantic relationships seem to have them in daylight as well as in the dark of a candlelight dinner. And they seem to maintain these relationships in the midst of life's hectic moments. Perhaps romance is not only found in the spectacular and the magical, but in those quiet, gentle times when we do things for each other that give us joy and create a bond that grows with time.

So, I've decided that romance can also be those things we do that make life easier because someone was thoughtful without any particular reason.

Many times, just before an evening meal, moments before my husband arrives home, I discover I am out of milk and bathroom tissue. There's no time to go to the store before he arrives. I hear the front door open and the dog jumping up and down. He's home! He walks in the kitchen carrying a grocery sack.

"You went to the store," I say (showing how perceptive I am!).

"Yeah," he says. I peek into the sack and there—you guessed it—milk and bathroom tissue!

"How did you know?" I asked.

"Just thought we might be out." (It had nothing to do with the fact that the bathroom copy of *Reader's Digest* had a lot of pages missing.)

We stand in the kitchen, holding milk and toilet paper, smiling at each other. That's romance.

You can just hang Hollywood and all of its pretty pictures of life, because this is *real life romance*, and I'll take it any day, any time! (And if he ever decides to send me flowers, I won't send them back!)

WHAT'S THIS THING CALLED REALITY?!

Children

$\mathscr{I}$ lay in bed trying to take the nap Momma thought I couldn't live without, looking wistfully through the screen windows of my mother and daddy's bedroom. Soft breezes through the room lifted the sheer, tied-back curtains, causing them to swing forward and back again. Sounds of Patricia, Charles Ray, and my brother Jim playing also drifted in and reminded me of all the things I was missing.

It was the summer of 1955 and my eighth birthday. School was out and I had successfully completed the year. I had performed in the school program as "The Old Woman Who Lived in a Shoe." You know the story—she had so many children, she didn't know what to do. Someone had built a giant-sized shoe, outfitted with windows and lovely country curtains.

I acted the part of Mother, scolding the children as they scurried in all directions, darting in and out of the house, or shoe as it were. All the children in my class sang a happy song, danced around as if we were celebrating this woman who had so many children, she didn't know what to do.

All the while, no one seemed to ponder why she had so many children. Obviously, she had wanted them. So, why wasn't she smart enough to know what to do? Was she old because she had so many children? Where did a lady go to get all those children? No one ever questioned the missing father or whether there had been a father at all.

I never considered that she might have been divorced. That word had not been introduced to my mind. Children of eight years of age in 1955 did not understand the "system" of getting children either. I knew where my two little brothers came from. On two separate occasions, my mommy and daddy had taken me to stay with another family. They had gone to the hospital and said that when they returned, I would have a baby brother or sister. I just figured it was sort of "pot luck" on babies at the Winchester, Tennessee, hospital. As it turned out, when my mommy and daddy got there, it was late at night and all of the little girls had already been taken by people who got there earlier in the day. There you have it — two baby brothers!

So, here I was, trying to will myself into a nap and wondering why I couldn't take them in the winter when there wasn't anything else to do anyway . . . and daydreaming at just what hospital I would pick up all my future babies. I drifted off to sleep hoping that I would know what to do with them.

Much later knowledge and truth connected. Knowledge that a mommy and daddy were necessary for making babies. The truth is that tons of millions of books have been written on the subject; and to this very day, no one can tell you exactly what to do with children.

Life is sharpened by a thing called reality. I was never blessed with the ability to have my own children. Perhaps I never found the right hospital. And when the year of my thirtieth birthday rolled around, I married a man with three children.

Our wedding had ended only moments before a stark reality hit me square between the eyes. The reception was filled with our favorite people, family, and food. We were having a wonderful time. Glancing around the room I caught three pairs of eyes staring at me. They were dark eyes, unlike my husband's light green ones. They were the eyes of the three boys—ages five, ten, and twelve—belonging to my brand new husband.

I broke out in a cold sweat. "Do you realize," I asked myself, "that you have just committed yourself to being partially responsible for these three boys for the rest of your life?"

"Yes," I said, once again to myself, "and thank the Lord they aren't girls. At least they'll never ask to borrow my clothes."

The father of these three and I had dated long enough that I had been allowed glimpses of what life would be like. Before we married, we were driving down the road one weekend in his Volkswagen Bug. Did you get that? His Volkswagen Bug. Small car. So small, it doesn't actually qualify as a car. But semi-intelligent people used to stuff their bodies into them. We were riding down the road with THREE boys in the back seat, the youngest of whom began to act up in a disruptive way. This man, the father of three boys, who is now my husband, corrected him and asked him not to do it again. (I was in the front seat being very quiet.) This small child, about five years of age, proceeded to run the same behavior by us again (in case we did not get the full impact the first time).

"Son," said the father, "if you do that one more time, I'm going to pull over and dust your behind in a way you won't forget!" (I'm still being quiet.) I have to hand it to this child— he had guts! He did "it" again. Before I could think "doodeley-do," the car was off the side of the road, the guilty child was being taken from the back seat, and the father and child were having a discussion and poof! They were both back in the car, and we were on the road again. The discussion apparently worked because the child did not do "it" again.

You can learn a lot from listening and being very quiet. We've been married a long time now, and I never get into an argument with my husband in the car.

This very same boy came to live with us when he was ten. A dear older lady said to me, "You just rear that boy with that wonderful sense of humor of yours and you'll do just fine."

I confess—there have been times that I couldn't remember having a sense of humor. Those were the times I thought I'd have to be put into a rehabilitation program just to learn to smile again. Fortunately there were other times when the sense of humor was alive and well. The day I carried five large bags of garbage from his room was not one of them. This young man is still breathing, due largely to the handcuffs his father bought which I frequently use to restrain myself.

Whether you acquire your children in an all-or-nothing package deal as I did, or carefully plan and give birth to children bearing your own stamp of heredity, there are many things that come as a complete shock. The volume of diapers a newborn can demolish in a day, for starters, can leave you with some doubt as to which end is up.

My Personal Gremlin

With the addition of children to my busy life I discovered that I have a personal gremlin following me around to cause humiliation and embarrassment. The gremlin keeps me humble and I shouldn't complain. But it seems that I've had more than my share of embarrassing moments.

The day I went out for an afternoon of shopping and covered most of the stores in town was one of them. I had visited at least fifteen places before a kind lady informed me that there was something hanging out the zipper of my skirt. The "something" turned out to be twelve inches of my slip. My zipper was in the back, and I had been shopping for hours wearing a long satin tail. Why me?

After years of incidents such as that one, I should have learned to take a long look in the full-length mirror before I walked out of the house. (But my life would be less eventful if I were that "together"!)

We went out for frozen yogurt one evening, and my husband came out of the yogurt shop shaking his head, looking just a little disgusted. He settled himself behind the wheel and handed me a cup of vanilla yogurt. I could see his mental wheels cranking so I waited before taking the first bite.

"There was a woman in there who looks like she pulled her sweat pants from the clothes dryer, put them on, and never noticed that six pairs of her husband's jockey shorts were stuffed in the behind. And there was something unidentifiable hanging out one leg. On top of all that, she wore a camouflage jacket. What woman in her right mind would go out in public dressed like that?"

"Did she have children with her?"

"Well, yes, she had three," he answered between bites.

"That explains it," I said. "She isn't in her right mind and won't be for years to come!" As we passed I glanced through the window of the yogurt shop and thought, just maybe, my personal gremlin had found a new home.

Only in the Movies . . .

If stress is the killer of romance and intimacy then stress should be spelled CHILDREN! If you listen to some people talk about looking forward to the joy of having children you realize they haven't been around any children for more than two or three minute stretches. In two minutes time a child can put both their best feet forward and leave a wonderful impression.

Some of these people sound like their children will just come poppin' into the world, six days later be fully grown and ready to select the perfect college.

The couple who maintains a satisfying, romantic, and intimate relationship with little ones careening around the house should be in *Guiness Book of Records*!

Their intimate moments must be like trying to make love in the center of Ringling Brothers Barnum & Bailey Circus. I can hear all your amorous young husbands saying, "It's OK, honey. Just relax — it's the end of the day — the children are asleep and there's nothing to interfere." Nothing, that is, except the fact that by the time he's finished his little discourse, she has fallen asleep with her head in the sink while brushing her teeth. His attitude isn't the only thing that's deflated; he's muttering something about it never ending this way in the movies.

The Bump in the Bed and Other Mysteries

Children will surprise you in many ways, not the least of which is coming into the world when you least expect them. When this happens the space you just remodeled into a computer and exercise room becomes the most expensive nursery in history. That's just the beginning of numerous surprises.

One morning you wake up in your new king-sized bed and notice a bump near the foot of it. "I didn't know we had a cat," you say.

"We don't," responds your husband. "It's your daughter. She sleeps like a cat. She crawled in under the spread after the lights were out."

It doesn't matter how many trips you make to put her back into her own bed. The bump in the bed will still be there when you wake up exhausted in the morning. The child, of course, wakes totally refreshed and doesn't remember how she got there.

An Eighteen-Month-Old and the Rock of Gibraltar

God wanted to keep us on our toes, so he wisely inserted into the aging process the time between eighteen months and three years of age. This proves that the Good Lord has a well-developed sense of humor. An eighteen-month-old child could shake the Rock of Gibraltar.

My brother, the doctor (the same brother who aged my thirty-nine-year-old mother to sixty overnight) now has two sons. (See, there is justice in this world.) As a physician, he has seen every crisis imaginable. Professionally, he is the very epitome of calm and mature control in all of the right ways. He *was*, that is, until his second child, at eighteen months of age, walked up to him smiling sweetly with brown juicy stuff oozing from his tiny mouth.

"Jarrod, what's in your mouth, Sweetie?" says his father the doctor. Jarrod continues to look rather pleased with himself and begins to chew vigorously with all of his eight teeth and gums. "Jarrod, come over here, little darlin', and let Daddy see what's in your mouth." Jarrod comes closer, Daddy picks him up and the fragrance hits: the faint but unmistakable fragrance of—yep—dog food! His daddy, the calm, mature doctor, begins to yell for help. "Susan, what in the samhill is this child doing with dog food in his mouth?" (Isn't it lovely how we always ask intelligent questions in a crisis?)

By now, Daddy has all ten fingers in Jarrod's tiny little mouth and is slinging dog food all over the room. The three-year-old brother is in a corner gagging. Dr. Daddy is pretty near hysteria. And little Jarrod is crying for all he is worth because Daddy took his dog food away.

Feeding Children Is Dangerous Business

You can always tell which adults have reared offspring. They're the ones who never sit down before they wipe off the chair.

My husband devised an interesting defense against flying food. Young children should only be fed while standing in a bathtub with no clothes on. In the summer, you can feed them outside and hose them down afterward.

There ought to be special liability insurance to cover all the suits and dresses ruined by flying food. Watching other people's children eat is sort of a hobby of mine. When we enter a restaurant, I always look around to get a fix on where the children are sitting (so I'll know where not to sit).

Children's eating habits fall into various categories, various chairs, carpets, hair, their ears, nose, etc.

There's the "one-by-each" eater. This is the neat one who picks up his peas with two fingers, one at a time. This eater takes three to four times longer to finish a meal, and it's safe to sit close to one of these types in restaurants.

Then there's the "ankle-biter," who not only refuses to eat, but makes sure his parents don't put a bite in their mouths either. If these parents do manage to shove something in this little person's mouth, it is blown full-force back into their faces. I never sit near these types of eaters because they can become bored with their parents and turn on total strangers.

The most deadly child is the "kamikaze eater." This child has the spirit of true joy and wants to share it with the world. They eat with both hands and take general aim in the direction of their mouths. These children probably end up as athletes. For every bite they eat, they slam dunk two bites over their heads, to the left or right and any other direction. Parents of these children can enjoy themselves when dining out, because these tots entertain themselves with food. *Never*, I repeat, *never* sit within thirty-five feet of one of these types of eaters.

If you have a child who combines all the eating characteristics — depending on their mood — the only suggestion I can make is that you invest in plastic clothing and only eat out with couples you don't care if you never see again.

However, if at all possible, you should never sit down to eat with anyone under eighteen years of age. Several years ago, I would have said with anyone under six, but because we are the proud parents of a seventeen-year-old male who still can't keep food on his plate, the age limit has gone up.

You Told Your Teacher What?!?

Just the sound of that phrase makes any parent break out in a cold sweat. "Telling all" is a problem usually restricted to children between birth and eight years. But the prime candidates are those little mouths between four and seven.

You may as well accept it. If you have a crisis of embarrassing proportions, or something you'd rather die than repeat, you can bet your bottom dollar (I've always wanted to see that dollar) that your little mouths will tell all they know.

They go beyond telling all they know. They tell *more* than they know! They spill their guts and a lot of other people's too. They tell the Sunday School teacher that Daddy slept on the sofa 'cause Mommy was mad. They tell the Sunday School teacher that Daddy was running around the house chasing Mommy, and Daddy got in big trouble because Mommy made Daddy go into her bedroom and stay there for a *long* time — and she stayed in there with him *just* to make him *mind*.

I know a pastor who would be *real* surprised to learn that his little motor mouth told her Sunday School teachers exactly what he "doesn't" sleep in at night.

THE RIPE 'OLE AGE OF CONFUSION

Adolescence

*C*anadian geese mate for life and, as far as anyone can tell, remain totally loyal and devoted until the death of their mate. But geese have several advantages over humans. Their children don't wear diapers, shave their heads, or ask for the keys to the car.

An adolescent trying to prove himself to be a fully-grown adult (or semi-adult) can look as awkward as an ostrich trying to dance Swan Lake. There are times you can't bear to watch, but are afraid not to.

One evening, our last remaining child at home reached the ripe 'ole age of fourteen. He walked into the bathroom, looking perfectly *normal* for a fourteen-year-old. He stayed in the bathroom for two and a half hours during which time he took it solely upon himself to shave off the hair over his ears.

My husband came into the bedroom and said, "Have you seen this boy's hair?"

"No, why?"

"Because a lot of it is missing," he said.

"You mean it fell out? No! I don't believe it," I said.

"I wouldn't believe it myself, except he's standing right there in the hall looking like he's been prepped for the electric chair."

I followed my husband into the hall. There stood a half-grown boy, looking like a pair of eyeballs wearing the biggest ears I'd ever seen.

This boy's father said, "Son, do you like to eat food?"

"Yes, sir."

"Do you like to sleep in this house in a real bed?"

"Yes, sir." His eyes by now were growing large.

"Then starting from this moment in time, this historic moment, your hair is officially growing and will be allowed to continue to grow until such time that you have a full head of it again. Do you understand me?"

"Yes, sir!"

You see, this hit the two areas where we couldn't lose. This child kept a spare pillow outside the refrigerator door so he could do the two things he loves most—eat and sleep.

Some parents lack the proper techniques necessary for parenting either a two-year-old *or* a teen-ager. It takes a delicate balance between being General Patton and Mother Teresa.

The problem in some families is that too many children take command of the authority in the home and don't relinquish it until age twenty-two or graduation from high school, whichever comes first.

Are We Sure Mom and Dad Did It This Way?

All of a sudden, I am able to relate to my own parents. I grew up in a home where we were allowed to have healthy, and a few unhealthy, heated discussions with our parents. All of us learned something: if our daddy believed in a principle, we could attack it from every imaginable angle, and we never got big enough or old enough to crack that belief.

I think my daddy cracked a few times, but the principles never changed. Now we just tell him that's the reason he has four strong-willed, tough-minded adult children who have principles that don't budge. Our children can rant and rave, pushing us close to a breakdown, but the principles never change.

At his worst moments he threatened us with "I'm gonna knock your block off." I wasn't real sure where my block was but felt pretty sure I couldn't sit down without it!

Daddy spent so much time with his brows knitted together that they finally grew together. He would mutter to himself, "I don't think I'll live through getting you raised." Honestly, I don't know how he did. But I am thankful that he allowed us to air our thoughts and show some emotion. He and Momma have survived rearing all four of us with at least one good brain between them remaining intact.

Think Fast and Take 'Em By Surprise!

A teen-ager is a person in the blooming stage. They are looking all around for a clue as to who they really are. Watching this transformation can be painful. It must be even more painful for those parents who don't think fast on their feet.

Our son came home from school sporting a new look, down to the Michael Jackson glove without the fingers that the singer had popularized.

"Want to tell me about the glove?" I asked him. It's always better to ask questions first.

"Well," he answered, "this is the new me!"

"What was wrong with the old you?"

"This is who I *really* am!" he said.

"Could I see the glove?" I asked.

He cautiously removed it and placed it in my hand. We were standing in the entrance to our home. So, I opened the front door and pitched that nasty thing outside. He was properly surprised!

"Explain this," I said. "If that glove is who you really are, I just threw you outside. But you seem to be standing here in front of me!"

He was speechless!

"Well," I said, "You'd better go outside and pick yourself up before the dog drags you off and buries you!"

That night around the dinner table we talked about "being who we really are." I complimented him for being a loving, warm person, and told him how unique he is "just as himself." We also said, "Son, there's no costume in the world that can improve on who you are as a person."

He never wore that glove again.

The Ragbag

Dressing a teen-ager today isn't what it used to be. Seems like a hundred years ago that the perfect wardrobe included matched sets of something or other. A skirt with the perfect sweater and loafers. Guys wore neatly pressed shirts tucked in at all the right places. Today, if you put one hundred teen-agers together in one place, you'd have what looks like a large yard sale hit by a small tornado.

Only a "nerd" wears clothes that fit. If the shirts aren't four sizes too big, they're "too small." If an outfit—both parts of it—matches, your child will promise you that no one will sit by him in the school cafeteria.

We spent good money on clothes to fit our high school junior. I drove all over town to find jeans the right length so he could tell me they were too short. So I drove sixty-five miles to return them and purchase jeans that are too long so the same teen-ager can roll up the legs until they are too short! Now he's happy.

We even bought all new socks so he could leave for school the next day with no socks, the pants legs rolled up, and his old tennis shoes on. But he was "cool."

The word cool is back. It was in during the sixties and lingered on, dying a slow death. Then it was — get this! — "totally uncool" to say "cool." Now tacky is cool—baggy pants that add forty-five pounds to your weight are in and you wear three shirts at a time (that's right), one over the other, in varying colors.

You can't give a teen-ager anything nice. Give him a perfectly good sweatshirt, and he'll cut the arms off, saying something truly profound like, "Now it's cool!"

There's Nothing New

I thought there could never be anything new under the sun. Yes, I *thought* so until last summer. We were depositing our son and his bike at the starting point for the youth group's Annual Bike Hike. I was standing to one side, minding my own business, doing what I love to do—watching people. When suddenly I zeroed in on a group of lovely teen-age girls preparing their bikes for the trip. I noticed that all the girls seemed to be wearing the same things.

Just what the things were, I couldn't quite identify, but I had to admit the "things" looked vaguely familiar.

"What in the name of peace are they wearing?" I asked our son.

"Shorts."

"Those don't look like shorts. They look like pieces of a sheet fabric held together by a large safety pin." The fabric didn't connect anywhere on the girls' bodies except at the waist.

"Mom, they're boxer shorts. They take their dad's boxer shorts and paint them. Cool, huh?"

"Yeah, cool."

I had an especially cool picture of the fathers of these little ladies running around their respective homes, searching for their boxer shorts.

The Truth Can Be Made Up If You Practice

During the Watergate hearings, there were grown men who employed a technique they no doubt borrowed from teen-agers. They *claimed* to have had blackouts. Their responses to questions concerning their activities would simply be, "I don't recall."

Our son may have been selling the right to use this excuse behind our backs, for I am quite sure he thinks *he* invented it. On one occasion, he committed several acts of disobedience around the house, all of which were obvious and left a telltale trail as to his activities while I was away, one of which was to spray my best cologne all over the house. After I recovered the ability to breathe, I summoned him downstairs.

"I would appreciate it if you would never again spray my cologne in the house," I said, "and you're not to rummage around in our bedroom when I'm away. Do you understand?"

"I haven't been in your room and I haven't sprayed your cologne," he responded.

When his father came home, we continued the discussion. This is a very creative child. He finally said he didn't remember if he had done all of these things. He said that he was having blackouts . . . blackouts!

We picked up on this phenomenon and began to discuss with each other how he must not be allowed on his bike again for fear he might have one of his "spells" and hurt himself. And how we would have to take him out of regular school, and first thing in the morning, we would call a specialist — one having to do with disorders of the brain. (Had he not been so clever, we would have thought he was missing one!)

About this time, a rather amazing thing happened. His memory began to return.

Teen-agers spend a lot of their waking hours proving that the truth *can* be made up. No one has ever convinced me exactly *why* they do this. My best hunch is that teen-agers are very creative thinkers—everywhere except in the classroom. Because of their creativity they feel the truth is much less intriguing than fiction. They also fictionalize because the truth often spells trouble with a capital T.

Our son came home from school one afternoon with a very colorful eye. It no longer matched his other one. It had a black ring around it.

"What happened to your eye?" I asked.

"What eye?" he responded.

"The one that's half shut and has a black ring around it like the dog on the old 'Little Rascals' show," I said.

"Oh, that. I ran into a door at school today," he replied without batting his other good eye.

"That must have been some door," I commented.

"Why?" he said

"Well, I've never seen one with a doorknob that high before!" He then proceeded to demonstrate just how he walked into a door frame (proving beyond a shadow of a doubt that our children think we're idiots).

When this child's father arrived home, I felt compelled to fill him in. "Your son got into a fight at school today and has a black eye," I stated.

"Oh, really?"

"Yes, and not only that, he actually thinks I believe he ran into a door."

Later, the chiid performed his "running-into-the-door routine" for his dad. It hadn't improved with time.

About this time, the phone rang. It was for the person sporting the black eye. He took it in the other room. The young fellow on the other end said, "Boy, you and Billy Roy sure got into big trouble, didn't you?"

I promise I was only listening to know when to hang up the phone. I put the receiver down. "Um," I said to my husband, "that's the first time I ever heard of a doorknob named 'Billy Roy'!"

The next call was from the school principal.

This same child brought home a report card showing grade averages that had fallen faster than the Dow Jones. We discussed the problem and possible solutions, which included selling his social life to the lowest bidder if things didn't get better. After an hour of this we realized we were flappin' our lips purely for the exercise, and that there was nothing but a warm breeze blowin' between his ears.

"Where in the world will we send this child to college if things don't improve?" I asked. "How about Bolivia?"

"Look Who's Embarrassing Whom"

Teens are embarrassed by everything their parents do in public, like breathing. One girl told her mother she was breathing "too loud!"

My husband's son hid under a rack of clothes rather than be seen shopping with his parents.

They will go out with you, but will never walk beside you. They walk four hundred yards behind or ahead of you until they need money. Then, they walk with their hands in your purse.

You can die of asphyxiation while your teen-ager experiments with finding the perfect fragrance to suit his personality. Our son's latest is "Ode d'Rambo," and I think I know why he's not dating.

We tried getting our teen-ager to share the household responsibilities. He offered to do the vacuuming. I should have known better. He vacuumed the same way he mows the yard—

he cuts down everything not planted in concrete. The first time he vacuumed, he sucked up the slipcovers off the sofa, three pairs of pantyhose, and the cat!

You have to be clever to be a parent these days. It helps to have a master's degree in thinking on your feet and a Ph.D. in gibberish, because you spend approximately twenty-three years per child deciphering it.

Teen-agers stay six steps ahead of you so they can occasionally look back to see if you're paying attention. Too many parents are rearing their children by the "ignore them til they go to college philosophy," and those parents, having lost their minds early on, never regain their sanity *or* their children.

FOURTEEN

THAT LAST STEP'S A TOUGH ONE

Stepparenting

*A*s I said earlier, I acquired all my children by marriage, and I don't recommend birth by that method. Children from previous marriages come pre-assembled. Their qualities are already firmly in place — the good, the bad, the ugly, and the lovely.

As in the fairy tales, stepmothers get all the blame and none of the credit. Who knows — maybe Cinderella had a sassy mouth we've never heard about!

If I ever had any illusions about being an easy-going person, they were quickly dispelled. Because I had never been a regular parent, stepparenting brought out emotions that made me think there might be mental illness in my background!

If you are a stepparent, you have to dissect every single word you say to the stepchild. In your sweetest voice you say, "Sweetheart, it would mean so much to me if you would go upstairs and clean your room. We're having company tomorrow, and we might just need to be able to get the door open, and it would be nice to see the floor again. OK?" And he gets angry.

But just let the child's real parent come home, and he or she can handle it like this. "You get your buns upstairs and clean your room, or I'm gonna know the reason why. Do you hear me?" "Yes, sir," he says and goes upstairs to do it.

There must be something to "knowing the reason why."

If you make one of these children cry, they'll tell their real parent, "*She* did it to me," with a look that says death row is too mild a sentence.

Stepparents are easy to identify. They're the ones with only half their teeth because they spend so much time grinding them. Some parental fears may not be so irrational for the stepparent: like fearing your children will grow up and live with you.

The only hope for parents in this situation is to stick together. *Always* back each other up—and not into a corner. It might be a good idea to ask your spouse to check on you every morning to be sure you lived through the previous day.

Some of you may be hanging on by your fingernails. To you I say, grow longer nails! You won't regret it. The best is yet to be.

Yours, Mine, or Whose?

Part of the joy that couples have in having their own children is that of seeing them grow and develop. Children who come from previous marriages reflect the values of someone with whom both you and your spouse may never agree.

These children are then forced to come and go between two separate homes where the expectations are vastly different. Children are flexible, but no human being alive can accept two value systems. They eventually will choose the values of one or the other and live by them.

Because I have lived with this type of situation, I take a tough stand on divorce. I believe it was never meant to be. But men and women are so fragile, so fallible, and often, just plain selfish and immature. Divorce too often is seen as the only alternative.

I take a hard stand when acquaintances of mine begin talking divorce. I say things like, "Consider the fact that someone you have yet to meet will marry your husband. They will influence the thinking of your children and their goals in life and may eventually spend more time with your children than you do."

My husband and I wish we had been married forever. We have been allowed to share such joy and closeness, but we are as honest with his children as we can possibly be. We talk about letting God plan their futures and letting God help them make major decisions.

The youngest child is the one who's lived with us full-time. I have cried for and with this child. I changed my life for him. I've fought with him and for him. I have been his greatest ally and worst enemy.

If you ask me what the most difficult task of my entire life has been, without pause, I will answer, "Rearing someone else's child."

He has taught me motherhood—the hard way. Yet he has been a joy. Without him, a large portion of this book would not exist. Without him, I would not be able to share with my friends the ins and outs of rearing children. Without him, my husband and I would have had fewer arguments, but also fewer laughs. I would look eight years younger and these two lines between my brows would not exist.

FIFTEEN

THE IN-LAWS
ARE COMING
The Other Family

*F*ortunately, like Mark Twain's death, reports on the horrors of in-laws, in a lot of cases, have been greatly exaggerated. I have never understood why in-laws have such a bad reputation.

I was having lunch with several good friends one day when one of them suddenly brought our fun to a close.

"I hate like everything to leave such good conversation, but I have to rush home and clean out my refrigerator."

"You're leaving this stimulating crowd to clean your refrigerator," I said, "how long have you had this problem?"

"Since I heard that my in-laws are coming tomorrow!"

"And your in-laws care what's in your refrigerator?" I asked.

"They not only care, they have notes on what's still there from the last time they visited!"

This opened a can of worms that we never quite got the lid back on. Everybody seemed to have a different tale, and it was amazing how much fun we had telling them.

One person picked up the conversation with, "When my mother-in-law comes to visit she wears her white gloves. She doesn't take them off until she has checked every square inch for dust. Then she doesn't say a word, just makes a clicking noise with her tongue, takes off the dirty gloves and leaves them in a prominent place."

Another said, "My father-in-law always comes to visit during the coldest days of winter. The first thing he does is stick his head up the chimney to check for soot build-up. Then he closes the fireplace doors while stating matter-of-factly that if we light one more fire in that chimney, the house will burn to the ground. So, our only choice is to freeze to death the entire time they're with us because we can't use the fireplace. Then he says, 'Son, I don't see how you stand this house; it's so dad-burn cold all the time.'"

I don't know where people go to find in-laws like this. Mine never seem to notice what's in the refrigerator. But I must admit to spending hours cleaning the oven and buying lots of groceries before my mother-in-law visits. Cooking is real important to her and whenever we see her she looks over her son from head to toe before saying, "Is she feeding you enough?"

These same in-laws have another title; when we have children, they become grandparents. Then just mark it down — it never fails — these same people who made sure you learned everything the hard way, who raised you not to be materialistic, who wanted you to appreciate the "value of things." These same people show up on your doorstep with every toy known to man, and a lifetime gift certificate to Toys R Us.

They can sniff out new-fangled gadgets for those grandchildren before they've even been invented.

After this stage in your relationship to in-laws and grandparents a new cardinal rule goes into effect: DON'T DARE SAY A CROSS WORD TO ONE OF THOSE LITTLE

DARLIN'S IN THE PRESENCE OF THE GRAND-PARENTS!

There's another rule that is close to being cardinal and it goes like this: Whatever the grandparent feeds the grandchild at dinner time is nutritious no matter what kind of junk food it is.

My mother is an experienced grandmother. She knows every trick and falls for every one of them. Her newest grandson was sitting happily in his highchair refusing to eat dinner the other night. She whipped out a bowl of ice cream and plopped it down in front of him. Naturally, he dug in with a fervor and cleaned up every last drop. Then smacked his little hand down and spoke, "More!"

"Isn't that cute?" she said as she went to the freezer for more!

The mother and father of this little piggy had a sort of green look on their faces, but they never said a word. They already knew the rules, and they knew that while you don't have to like them, you do have to play by them.

"In-Laws — Out-Laws — in Love"

"I'm as nervous as a cat passin' a dog pound."

"What's there to be nervous about?" he asked me.

"Meeting your parents . . . especially your father."

"He's harmless — trust me!"

"He sounds like a character to me," I answered.

"Well, when you two meet, it'll just be two characters meeting each other . . ."

So, I took a deep breath and opened the door to meet my future father-in-law for the first time. He said, "Hi, Sugh! Where's the sofa?" Then he went to the sofa and took a nap, while the rest of us carried on without him.

You have to admit it's an odd stroke of timing that just when we've begun to make peace with our own parents after all the preadult trauma of growing up, we marry and acquire another set of parents to contend with!

All those mother-in-law stories make me ill. Like the one where the couple is passing through a town, sees a huge crowd gathered around the square. The man pulls over to find out what all the commotion is about.

"What's going on?" he inquires.

"Well," drawls the 'ole country gentleman, "Jed Bleckers' mule kicked his mother-in-law in th' head and killed her!"

"Then this here's a memorial service."

"Shoot naw, this here's an auction; ever' man in town wants to buy that mule."

These sorts of stories don't apply to my mother-in-law. But I will say this. There is at least one thing that mothers and mothers-in-law have very much in common! They can inspire guilt quicker than the ten commandments! After all, what's the use of going through all the trouble of raisin' children if you can't have the pleasure of makin' them miserable once in a while after they're grown!

My father-in-law was in some ways infuriatingly uncompromising. In other ways, he was merely delightfully unusual! My mother-in-law referred to them as the "Princess and the Pea." Off they would go to the opera or symphony — she, dressed to the nines, he outfitted in his bib overalls and a full-length black opera cape. (Believe me, this fact can be substantiated!) This man was so unusual that I thank my lucky stars my own husband wears a Ralph Lauren jacket instead of overalls.

My father-in-law was affectionately known as "Pappy." In his later years he slept a lot. We practically had to move the dining room table to the sofa so he could do the two things he loved most — eat and sleep. He and his adolescent grandson had a lot in common.

I don't know how in the world my mother-in-law managed to "hog-tie" Pappy the day of our wedding. But I'm sure that's what she did. He showed up wearing a pair of dress slacks, a jacket complete with a dress shirt and no tie. I was all geared up for him to come in his overalls and to charm everyone with one of his many tales. I was disappointed. Being in "dress clothes" brought out his crotchety side, which was always lurking dangerously near the surface anyway.

When he came to my baby sister's wedding he wore his overalls but refused to stay for the reception. He did make a dramatic sweep through the crowd "just to give these folks the pleasure of havin' a look at me." Then with a "goodbye Sugh" and a brief hug he and mom were on their way.

Pappy's schoolin' ended with the ninth grade, but he was one of the best educated people I've ever known because he read. He knew more history than Henry Kissinger and could recite human interest stories like Will Rogers.

When he told one of his "good" jokes, Mom would laugh like she hadn't heard it three hundred times before. When he slipped in a "bad" one she gave him one of those looks only married people understand.

Pappy Went to Church — Sometimes!

Pappy went to church with mom once every few months whether he needed it or not. When he did, he dressed up a bit. He figured that God at least deserved his white bib overalls. He'd slip in and sit on the very back pew, 'cause he didn't believe in getting too close to the preacher in case the sermon got a little "firey." And he thought it made good sense to be near a door in case it stretched on too long.

He was never one to be comfortable in crowded places. I can't say how he's makin' out in heaven, but, God bein' God n'all, probably has a special section for the "overall" gang, and it most likely has a lot of elbow room.

He wasn't an easy man to live with and no one knew it better than he! But my mother-in-law loved him and he adored and loved her.

She stuck it out through the tough years and there were plenty of them. She was looking forward to their fiftieth wedding anniversary, and they were just a few months shy of it when the Good Lord called him home. I stood beside her during the weeks when Pappy was slippin' away. She left his side only at night to go home and sleep so she could return again the next day.

I saw a love in her face that revealed both the joy and anguish of years spent living with him. It was a love so deep some folks today wouldn't be able to fully comprehend it. Her love cradled him until the end when she was forced to say goodbye and let him go.

When the end of their lives together came I walked out in the corridor of the hospital and thought, "Some people give up on marriage before they collect enough memories."

THREE SHADES
OF GREEN
Jealousy

I saw that!"

"What?" he asks.

"I saw you look at that woman in that car!"

"WHAT Woman in WHAT car?" he demands, sounding as if he had no earthly idea what I was talking about.

"The woman sitting in the car at the corner! I saw you lookin' her over!"

"I was not looking at *any* woman in *any* car on *any* corner!"

"I didn't say just *any* woman, I said THAT woman; and you know good n' well which woman I'm talking about!"

"For your information, I was looking at that uprooted tree on the corner lot! Get a grip on yourself."

"You were looking at an uprooted tree," I restated (I read somewhere that it's a good idea to restate something when you can't believe your ears!).

"Right! . . . A tree!"

"What color hair did it have?" I said.

"This conversation is over!"

The first thing I did the next morning was get my car out of the garage and point it in the direction of THAT corner lot. I eased up to the stop sign, turned my head in the general direction of the empty lot, and there it was—the most gigantic mass of roots (and NOT the kind on a bleached blond) I've ever seen. That tree had swayed in its last breeze and spread its final shade. It was lying there bottom side up, naked and embarrassed for all the world to see.

Even my car seemed to be reprimanding me as I turned around to kick myself all the way home. Tell you the truth, this was one incident in our married life that left me too embarrassed to mention again. The next time my husband and I drove by *that corner*, he cleared his throat three times and stared in my direction. I never took my eyes off the road, but I could see him smiling through the corner of my eyes. I got the message. It's bad enough when I make an idiot out of myself, but when I do it in front of him it's called humiliation!

Jealousy is powerful—powerful and "usually" irrational. It is powerful because it has the potential for destroying relationships. Irrational because so often we let wild imaginings rule our thinking. When we succumb to our suspicions, we become the victims of our own thoughts. Experts on the workings of the human mind and emotions tell us that our minds do not differentiate between a "perceived" danger and a "real" danger. When we "perceive" something as a threat, our body responds by producing all the extra chemicals and hormones to carry us through the danger. Unfortunately, all of us are capable of thinking our way into quite a state of confusion and chaos. Jealousy is an emotion where this definitely applies.

"If You Could See You Now . . ."

Jealousy is a game some couples play. These are the couples who seem to take it upon themselves to inspire jealousy by hanging all over other people's spouses at parties. Beneath this kind of behavior usually lies a low self-image that needs constant bolstering by trying to appeal to the "masses." They dangle their flirtations in front of each other like a seductive lure. They may even use these situations later as emotional blackmail. You know, the "I saw you and so and so . . ." routine.

If these types of couples could have an out-of-body experience and see themselves as others see them, it wouldn't look so attractive. They would see jealousy for what it is — embarrassing. They might see it as immaturity, insecurity, and self-centeredness in action.

There's a phenomenon that occurs in the male species and it can, I said *can,* cause jealousy if we are so inclined to *let* it. It is called *looking.* Just the act I accused my husband of doing at the famous corner lot! Men do look! That's not the phenomenal part of it though; they look and then they usually deny it!

If you are of a temperament inclined toward feelings of jealousy, this characteristic can take you on a quick trip to hysteria. Looking is harmless when it does not include *leering.* The act of looking should consist of merely a quick glance in the general direction of someone, anyone. But the act of *leering* is dangerous. It carries with it the connotation of more than a *passing* interest and could be interpreted as lust.

Men don't have a lock on the market of leering. I've been in the company of women who go out of their way to leer at an attractive person of the opposite sex. As I've said, it's a strange phenomenon. We get married and commit to fidelity forever and ever, but permit our eyes to occasionally take little side trips. It's the *motive* behind those "little side trips" that can be innocent or dangerous.

My husband recently took me to see a Tom Selleck movie. It was delightful. Mr. Selleck never looked better and his acting wasn't bad either. The movie ended and as the credits were disappearing I mumbled, "Tom Selleck is absolutely adorable." That's innocent enough, don't you think? I looked at my husband and found him staring at me with one of those famous looks that was laced with more than a little bit of jealousy — and he wasn't saying anything — just staring.

I started covering my bases pretty fast. "You're adorable, too, and handsome. In fact, I've never noticed it before but you look a lot like Tom Selleck."

He just shook his head in amazement as we got up from our seats. He was still shaking his head as we got in the car. So, I asked him about it, and he said to get used to it because he expects to spend the rest of his life shaking his head in amazement.

Another Shade of Green

I experienced another kind of jealousy several years ago after receiving a letter from a friend I had not heard from in years. Her husband was perfect. His job was perfect. Her children were the vision of perfection. They were gorgeous. They were not only athletic — they excelled! All their pimples were in hidden places. They were brilliant. They were talented, and not just in one area! They sang, danced, and played instruments. T-H-E-Y — made me nauseous.

She concluded her five-page commercial for herself with, "Please write and tell me about yourself." That letter lies unanswered in my box of keepsakes. I've kept it all of these years because I have never known anyone so *perfect* and that letter may be worth a lot of money if Ripley's Believe It Or Not ever comes back on the air.

I did compose one line: "I almost had children, but God took one look down here and kept them. He said there was absolutely no place on this earth for *perfect angels*." Jealousy is to a marriage what a too-tight girdle is to a very large person, or a shoe that's several sizes too small on a good-sized foot — painful!

Jealousy is an emotion that gives us permission to make blithering idiots of ourselves and never even notice. This was the case with a wife who was so jealous of her husband she called around all day, following his trail like a coon hound, just to be sure he was where he said he was. This guy wasn't fooled for a second. He began leaving a fake itinerary on the kitchen counter to keep her guessing.

The case of the husband who was into gadgets is a very contemporary one. He was so positive his wife was having an affair that he gave her a personal pager so he could at least interrupt her romantic interludes. She got three pages in the middle of the supermarket.

I will even admit to a recurring jealousy of an unknown woman! I feared that my husband would outlive me, marry someone else who would take over my clothes, and use all my things, not the least of which was my husband.

I have told him in no uncertain terms that if he does marry again, my skinny little ghost will come back and "hover" over him! But my greatest fear is no longer that he will outlive me; it is that somehow he will get a copy of this book and read it!

Jealousy causes us to miss out on a lot of life. Because the emotion of jealousy is one of self-absorption we focus on what we *think* we see rather than what is actually happening. Not only do we miss out on moments we may never recapture, we expend considerable energy cleaning up the mess our jealousy creates—the miscommunication, hurt feelings, resentment, doubt of ourselves and spouses. It finally comes down to this: it isn't worth it.

Turn your attention to some other "irrational fears" that in the long run may not be so irrational. I'll give you some ideas to take your mind off jealousy: the fear of becoming pregnant on your twenty-fifth wedding anniversary, and the thought of having a preschooler who is learning to read at a time when you can't read a word without bifocals! Think of this one for a while—the thought of having a child in little league when at your age, aerobic exercise means bending down and trying to get back up. Imagine attending PTA meetings at the time you get a notice in the mail that you may now apply for your AARP Card (American Association of Retired Persons).

Experts tell us that only about seven percent of all the things we fear will ever *possibly* come to pass. Now, we have something new to fear—spending the rest of our lives trying to figure out which of our fears will become the seven percent.

God knew that man was prone to irrational thinking. Because of this He gave us some guidelines in His Word. He said, "Fix your thoughts on what is true and good and right . . . and think on these things."

Spend a few years passing every thought by that verse and you will find the fears being replaced by truth, goodness, and a healthy picture of reality.

HAPPILY EVER "AFTERWORD"

*T*he only kind of divorce allowed in our house is when we are in separate rooms, mad at each other. On one of these occasions, my husband blurted out, "I want a divorce. I've had it!" And he walked out of the room into the sunroom, muttering that he would sleep there for the night.

"You can't get one," I yelled after him, "because I want one first!" I promptly turned, stormed into the living room, and slammed the door.

After five very quiet moments passed, I felt a strange thing happen in my stomach that worked its way up and into a laugh as I realized the total absurdity of this situation. Sheepishly, I walked through the house. The old pine floors crackled as I walked. They seemed to be laughing, too.

I reached the sunroom. My six-foot-one husband was stretched out on the wicker loveseat, arms and legs hanging off in every direction. He took one look at me and a giant-sized grin overcame his face. I took one look at him and began to giggle. He laughed. I laughed.

"I wish we could bottle this," I said.

"Bottle what?" he asked.

"The ability to laugh at ourselves and know when we're being stupid—just stupid, stupid, stupid," I replied. We laughed all the way back to our bedroom.

We take our marriage seriously and because we do, we laugh every chance we get.

Laughter is the ingredient that lifts us to the lighter side of life. Performing comedy these past years has taught me a new truth. We should not take ourselves too seriously. It's other people we should take seriously, only occasionally granting that attention to ourselves. It's to this end that this book is written.

Marriage Is Funny Business

Marriage is funny business. If you haven't noticed, you haven't been looking in the right places. Or perhaps you can't see the funny because there are some grim realities clouding your view.

Remember, the very same mirror that reflects a clear image becomes coated with grime when left unattended—grime that first obscures and then totally blocks the view.

When we married each other, my vision was clouded with love and passion, and all I could see were my husband's finer qualities. He was wonderful and full of humor and strong. I liked his mind and the way he put words together when we talked. His eyes were green and his beard had no gray. He knew things I didn't, and I let him share them with me. I knew things that he didn't, and he appreciated that knowledge. We talked about everything from A to Z.

As time passed, my vision remained clouded, but not with stars in my eyes. There have been times when the circumstances of our lives were tough—really tough. At one point, I realized I was no longer focusing on all those wonderful, charming traits and qualities that had attracted me to my husband in the first place. Rather than seeing the good, I only saw the negative. And a very unfunny thing happened: I began to feel dissatisfied and unhappy. Often my sentences began, "If you only . . ."

Feelings of resentment came between us. Our conversations were no longer something we looked forward to. I began to find him less attractive. He no longer told me how special I was. We didn't laugh any more. There was no joy. A home with no joy is like a home with no air—you can't breathe and you want to escape.

But walking away from the marriage was not an option for us. We *chose* to stop the negative thinking. I *chose* to see the good and pray about the rest. I asked him to forgive me for complaining. He asked me to forgive him for become angry. We began to say good things to each other again. We worked *hard* to walk our way back to each other emotionally and the reward was worth it.

We worked hard and we were lucky. It's a sad fact that too many marriages are like a boat with a slow leak. You know they are going to go down—it's just a matter of when. I believe in plugging the holes from the inside out.

Plugging the holes from the inside out results in a marriage that deals with life's crises as they come along, a marriage that endures past the point of no return and doesn't recognize the meaning of the word quit. A marriage that plugs the holes from the inside out is well acquainted with commitment. Here's hoping you have located the weak spots in your marriage and will be committed to repairing them.

We're all working on a Ph.D. in life—the living of it. Life has knocked me down a number of times, but fortunately I've the ability to look at life a bit lopsided and come up laughing. Through this book we have shared a personal celebration of marriage. This book has provided a glance through the skin of marriage—a look below the surface, where the relationship is lived out with laughter and tears.

It Helps to Have a Sense of Humor

In writing this book, I've discovered I have some strange writing habits, but they work. For some reason I'm inspired by being around people. So for a couple of hours after taking our son to school, I stopped by Jay's Donut Junction to have my coffee and write. It's a local meeting place in the mornings—warm and friendly, with free refills on coffee. People come in for that "wake-me-up" cup and read the morning paper while munching on freshly-made donuts that truly are made while we sleep.

In this casual atmosphere I can park myself on the edge of a less-than-comfortable straight-back chair and perfect the art of acquiring writer's cramp in a place far below my hand. One particular morning, as the lady behind the counter refilled my cup, she wanted to know what kind of book I was writing. "A humorous book on marriage," I told her. She laughed and said, "Well, it sure helps to have a sense of humor when you've been married thirty-five years like I have." (I found out later she became pregnant with her one and only child the year of her twenty-fifth anniversary—tell me that doesn't take a sense of humor.)

The customer standing beside me interrupted in a rather brusk voice and said, "Marriage ain't funny at all when you've just been walked out on after ten years of it." After seconds of silence, I said, "I'm not writing about divorce because your right; there's not one thing funny about it. I am writing with the hope that if there are some homes where the bags are already packed, the clothes will find their way back into the closet."

So, there you have it. I have written about marriage. I have written with the hope that if we can endure each other's idiosyncrasies and even learn to laugh at them, there will be more couples married beyond recognition, for whom walking out is nothing more than exercise. Good laughter makes us humble. I am not talking about the kind of laughter that be-littles someone else, but instead the shared dignified laughter that reminds us of who we really are. And puts a smile on the realities we're dealing with. So, here's to laughter. And to love. May both grace your marriage and your life.

The Last Word

"The book is finished!" I said as we were getting into bed.

"Does this mean you won't be sleeping with pencils in your hair any more?" he asked.

I gave him a funny look. (He had one already but I didn't give it to him!) "I love you," I said, "and guess what?"

"I love you, too, and what is it now?"

"I'm having the last word. Good night!"

Silence.

And we go to sleep smiling.

Together.

COLOPHON

The typeface for the text of this book is *Baskerville*. Its creator, John Baskerville (1706-1775), broke with tradition to reflect in his type the rounder, yet more sharply cut lettering of eighteenth-century stone inscriptions and copy books. The type foreshadows modern design in such novel characteristics as the increase in contrast between thick and thin strokes and the shifting of stress from the diagonal to the vertical strokes. Realizing that this new style of letter would be most effective if cleanly printed on smooth paper with genuinely black ink, he built his own presses, developed a method of hot-pressing the printed sheet to a smooth, glossy finish, and experimented with special inks. However, Baskerville did not enter into general commercial use in England until 1923.

Substantive editing by George Grant
Copy editing by Stephen Hines
Cover design by Kent Puckett Associates, Atlanta, Georgia
Typography by Thoburn Press, Tyler, Texas